RESPONSIVE THERAPY

RESPONSIVE THERAPY
A Systematic Approach to Counseling Skills

Sterling K. Gerber, Ph.D.
Eastern Washington University
Cheney, Washington

HUMAN SCIENCES PRESS,INC.
72 FIFTH AVENUE
NEW YORK, N.Y. 10011

031701

Printed in the United State of America
987654321

Library of Congress Cataloging-in-Publication Data

Gerber, Sterling K.
  Responsive therapy.

  Includes index.
  1. Counseling. 2. Psychotherapy. 3. Psychiatry—
Differential therapeutics. I. Title.
BF637.C6G45   1986   158'.3   85-21869
ISBN 0−89885−267−6
ISBN 0-89885−269−2 (pbk.)

CONTENTS

FOREWORD

This work is the culmination of two trends. The first is a move to present therapy skills in a marketable form to younger students. In years past, counseling and psychotherapy were the province of graduate programs. It was usual to encounter formal therapy training sometime during the master's program, usually after considerable cognitive preparation. Realizing that the skills of therapy, like other skills, could be introduced without a thorough conceptual foundation and brought to a higher level of perfection through a longer period of coached practice, some training programs instituted an immediate and continuous practicum experience for graduate trainees.

Wishing to increase the proficiency of graduate counselors by providing even more coached practice, the Applied Psychology Department at Eastern Washington University moved the beginning therapy skills class to the senior year of its undergraduate program. This provided more extensive training for the talented student, allowed some experiential data for professors and students to use in assessing probable success in a therapy training program, and provided usable skills for bachelor's degree holders to use in a variety of entry-level people-helping jobs.

In order to move the generally uninitiated student immediately into acquisition and practice of therapy skills, two things are necessary. First, the skills need to be embedded in a philosophical framework that provides for direct application of those skills in a practical form. Second, a statement of the philosophy and skills in fairly complete yet rudimentary form is required to provide the students with an understanding of the skills and their usefulness.

The second trend that gave rise to this work is a little more complicated to explain. Some historical information will help explain it.

In its infancy the counseling profession was concerned with ascertaining client abilities and matching them to occupational demands. The counselor who was knowledgeable in assessment methods and aware of work requirements was in a key position to diagnose and prescribe.

The same process was readily generalized to school guidance program needs and psychological treatment programs. Clients, who were deficient in some regard, sought consultation with counselors, who were wise and sensitive and could direct the clients toward proper adjustment.

As a natural parallel, the testing movement fit very well into this assessment-diagnosis-prescription model of therapy. This model formed the basic structure for E. G. Williamson's directive therapy (1939, 1950, 1958, 1965, Williamson & Bordin, 1941), popularized in his writings in the 1940s and into the 1960s.

As is typical of the dynamics of strong advocacy, where one position is countered by an opposing one, approaches having differing philosophical bases and contrasting with Williamson's approach were developed. The most prominent oppositional system was labeled nondirective therapy (now called person-centered therapy) by its principal advocate, Carl Rogers (1942). His system was based on the premise that people possess the capability of solving their own problems if provided an atmosphere conducive to objective self-awareness and positive support—conditions natural to people but distorted or perverted by societal practices. Unconditional positive regard, warmth, and empathy on the part of the counselor toward the client provided a climate that was facilitative of self-directed, progressive behavior on the part of clients (Rogers, 1961).

With such seemingly dichotomous systems competing for the allegiance of neophyte therapists, it was predictable that intermediate approaches would be created. Among these was a truly middle-ground approach, called eclectic therapy, advanced by Frederick Thorne (1950, 1961).

Eclecticism is the process of selecting what is considered best from different systems or sources and favoring no particular belief or practice. Although this notion appealed to many counselors as the only defensible system, it had two perceived weaknesses: (a) it required diagnosis as a prior accomplishment to selection of the best approach, which was contrary to the nondirective philosophy; and (b) it advocated the use of techniques disembedded from their philosophical and theoretical contexts.

In a very pragmatic sense, using techniques outside their philosophical context should be okay. If it works, why not use it? The problem occurs when techniques, demonstrated to be effective in one context, are combined with other contextually useful techniques, with the assumption that the combination will work. One example of a counterproductive, eclectic combination was an attempt to "humanize" a strong contingency-management program in an institution for delinquent youth. The result was the application of emotional reinforcers at the same time as the withholding of privileges or rewards. Acting-out behavior was simultaneously being reinforced and extinguished; unconditional positive regard and warmth do not necessarily complement a behavior modification format. Some combinations are obvious enough to be avoided. Others may involve less discernible counterproductive aspects.

During the 1950s students of counseling were offered, in essence, three choices: directive therapy, nondirective therapy, or eclectic therapy. For those who viewed eclecticism as a perversion of methods and hence misdirected and probably counterproductive, there were only two choices. As a result, students who could comfortably become disciples of Williamson or Rogers did so, and most others called themselves eclectic for want of a better label.

Without tracing the philosophical or theoretical genealogy

of each, the either-or, to-diagnose-or-not-to-diagnose kinds of dynamics have resulted in a plethora of counseling approaches, each with its proponent and disciples and each claiming to be a little closer than all the others to "truth." Some examples of contemporary therapies are neo-Freudian (Ford & Urban, 1963), Ellis and rational-emotive therapy (1969), Berne and transactional analysis (1961), Perls and Gestalt (1969), Wolpe and behavioral therapy (1973), Glasser and reality therapy (1965), Lowen and bioenergetics (1975), biofeedback (Birk, 1973), and humanistic counseling (Sutich & Vich, 1969).

There remains the temptation of eclecticism as a means of resolving the "duty" to choose an approach, but it still suffers from the fractionating and invalidating problem resulting when methods are administered out of context.

The process of discipleship, of adopting a particular model as best or most comfortable, results frequently in emphasizing those factors that make that model different from and better than others. Some people focus on similarities across models or on matching therapeutic approach to client style.

Fiedler (1950) drew the conclusion that accomplished therapists across identity lines were more similar than were new and more experienced therapists within the same therapeutic emphasis. Combs and Soper (1963) asserted that there are critical perceptual skills common to proficient therapists without regard to theoretical identity; these skills included the tendency to perceive from an internal rather than an external frame of reference and the preference to organize around people rather than things. Studies supporting the notion that some clients, because of their unique personalities, are helped more readily if matched to counselors with similar styles (Berenson & Carkhuff, 1967) and inferences that well-known therapists attract clients who are more apt to "fit" their preferred approach suggest a differential worth of therapeutic approaches.

An overview of this history suggests a theoretical dialectic struggle. One position is established (thesis); a different and seemingly opposing model is created (antithesis); eclecticism offers a middle ground which presumably extracts the best from its polar antecedents (synthesis). The second trend, from a backdrop of the previous description of history, is a move toward a theoretical ecumenism—a move from an "either/or" way of thinking to an attitude that incorporates "both."

There are basically three themes developed in this book. The first, treated early for foundation and in the last chapter for completeness, is a theoretical matrix for inclusion of the other two and as a platform for student cognitive development.

The second theme focuses on characteristics of effective therapy and skills for its management. Those skills are organized into a framework of sequential initiating, tracking, and enhancing (SITE) skills. Examples and practice exercises are included.

Given the possibility that the various therapy models are little else than varying views of the same reality or may be selectively accurate views of different portions of the same reality, it would be possible to incorporate all of them into one grand scheme. This is the third theme. It is developed in four chapters that provide the rational structure, brief descriptions of many models organized into "family groups," and an extended description with examples of a representative model from each of three groups.

Particularly influential in the preparation of this book were those professors who, more than 20 years ago, sensitized me to the disciple-eclectic dilemma. For the past 12 years Dr. Dick Sampson and I have worked closely together in refining the SITE skill approach. It would be impossible to separate his input from mine, and the skills presentation owes much to his influence and contribution.

Extensive quotes from works of Albert Ellis are used by permission of the Institute for Rational-Emotive Therapy.

Credit must go also to my wife, Laurelle, for her aid in preparing and proofing the manuscript, and a special thanks to Richard Greinert for the in-text graphics.

All names and other identifying information have been fictionalized throughout the text. Resemblance to any persons, living or dead, is not intended.

Chapter 1

INTRODUCTION

"What kind of a therapist are you?"

"A good one!"

"No! I mean, are you Adlerian, Rogerian, Skinnerian? Do you emphasize Gestalt, rational-emotive, transactional analysis, bioenergetics, or what?"

Such a dialogue is common among sophisticated and not so sophisticated counselors, therapists, and mental health specialists. It may even occur between a prospective client and therapist. There is an assumption in such an interaction that one cannot be therapeutic without identifying with a prominent movement. But it's common knowledge that ministers, bartenders, hairdressers, friends, and even strangers can be therapeutic.

What does a trained therapist do that is different from what the neighbor does? What does a Freudian therapist do that differs from a Rogerian therapist?

Part of the answer is "nothing." The dynamics of being therapeutic are the same across many clients and many helpers. Presumably a trained therapist is more sensitive and more efficient in managing those dynamics than is a neighbor or bartender. Presumably also, therapists with differing labels employ selected techniques in unique ways.

Three levels of therapy seem to be implied in the above statements. The first is where nonprofessionals perform in therapeutic ways, perhaps accidentally or through common sense. The second level assumes that all therapists share similar techniques that promote client progress and prepare the way for more specialized techniques. The third level is that of the therapist who manifests skills in accordance with a specialized, theoretical approach typically referred to by titles such as Gestalt, behavior modification, and so on.

For students of therapy, learning the middle-level skills, those common to all good therapists, is extremely important. It can be postulated that an extremely effective therapist is one who has some natural ability and interest (like the "therapeutic" minister or bartender or neighbor), a solid foundation in the universal skills, and some specialized training in one of the "name" therapies.

The emphasis of this book is on preparation in the universal or foundation skills embedded in a model or theory of counseling which is compatible with advanced study in a number of counseling models. Some attention now will be given to support for the middle-level or foundation skills.

A Common Thread in Therapies

Studies such as Fiedler's (1950) and those reported by Berenson and Carkhuff (1967) and Combs and Soper (1963) provide support for the notion of similarities across approaches by therapists who are effective. Descriptions by therapists of their unique approaches occasionally describe or imply preparatory skills. For example, in the study of some materials on reciprocal inhibition (Wolpe 1973, 1978; Yates 1970) some ideas appeared to be incongruent with stereotypical notions of a behavioral approach. Contrary to the presumed "formula" nature of elaborating a fear hierarchy and systematically proceeding through visualizations, some statements relating to the individuality of and variations among clients were made. Procedures such as the introductory interview, history taking, relaxation training, and hierarchy establishment were described dynamically as similar in some respects to other kinds of therapy. At one point, when suggesting studies comparing nonbehavioristic therapies with behavioral counseling, Wolpe (1978) wrote, "Any comparative study, to be satisfactory, would have to allow for the inadvertent therapeutic effects that all psychotherapies share" (p. 443).

In addition, then, to potential differential effects of contrasting theories, there apparently are common or similar elements that have therapeutic effects across theoretical lines. Some obvious similarities would include faith in the therapist, desire to "get better," investment of money and effort in the process, and prediction of positive change. These are conditions that a client brings to any counseling experience and that tend to support its success.

In addition to similarities that clients bring to therapy, there is a portion of the successful counseling process common to all therapies and, hence, atheoretical. Dynamics supporting the initial interaction, during which time (a) a relationship is established, (b) problems are identified and/or elaborated, and (c) objectives become established, are similar—whether or not prior testing has been done, whether or not a diagnosis has been made, and whether or not the presenting problem is at all related to the real therapeutic objective.

A careful analysis of these dynamics makes it possible to begin all therapy in very much the same way, work to identify the "real problem," ascertain the style of the client, and find the available options for treatment.

THEORY BASE

Responsive therapy relies very heavily on the universal, common skills. These skills permit the therapist to initiate and manage the counseling interaction and yet maintain enough conceptual and process flexibility to give clients the freedom to communicate their style and circumstance.

In other words, the therapist is most knowledgeable regarding the counseling process and must "teach" the clients how to use that process in a beneficial manner. The clients are most knowledgeable about themselves but usually have not organized that knowledge in a manner necessary to find a solution to their dilemmas.

The early stages of therapy require the counselor to establish and enhance communication from the client without getting in the way of or distorting either the flow or the direction of client output.

One concept that is necessary in understanding the dynamics of the therapeutic interview is phenomenal space. Each individual experiences and interprets reality in a unique way, and the results of those experiences and interpretations cannot be shared directly with another person. Two people may agree on the label for a common referent or object, but there is no way to verify commonality. Take, for example, two people viewing a bright red flower. How can either know that what is experienced is identical to the experience of the other? Given the case of one person who is to some degree color-blind but has learned to label the object in the appropriate way, it is almost a certainty that his/her experience is not the same as that of a person with normal color vision.

The client is the only person who has access to his/her own phenomenal space. Given the opportunity and structure, the client can and usually will describe the most salient features of that phenomenal world.

Therapy is a teamwork concern wherein the client attempts to explain or describe that unique phenomenal world; the counselor, in attempting to clarify and understand, causes the client to describe more completely, more accurately. Both client and counselor achieve an increasingly clear awareness of "what is happening" to, for, or with the client.

If the therapist is overpowering in manner, the client may say what he/she thinks is supposed to be said. If the therapist has to generate questions, those questions and their pattern of organization will come from the counselor's phenomenal space and may show very little correspondence to what is in the client's world.

Of first importance to the therapist is initiating a pattern of interaction in which the client talks and the therapist understands. This is accomplished by using the first skills in the sequential initiating, tracking, and enhancing (SITE) skills pattern.

Obviously it is possible for a client to talk about insignificant things from his/her phenomenal space. The important thing at first is the pattern of information being generated by the client. As the process gets going, progressively more important data will be elicited.

As the process continues, the client discloses two kinds of messages: problem and style. The problem, or set of circumstances, becomes defined through a series of communication levels. The style is demonstrated by the manner in which the client proceeds through those levels. Some examples of style are a tendency to think abstractly, reliance on intuition, orderly thought pattern, focus on feelings, aggressiveness and insensitivity (bull in china shop), concern for others, hypervigilance (looking for cues from therapist), and so on. How the client deals with therapy and the therapist is a cue for the manner of dealing with problems and with other people.

Relative to the problem or set of circumstances, the client must be tracked through the communication levels. These can be visualized as an inverted triangle (two dimensionally) or as a funnel (three dimensionally) (Figure 1-1).

At the top of either visualization is talk about the person. The most words and least meaning occur in verbalizations sprinkled with slang words and phrases and with connotative language. They contain suggestions of meanings other than or beyond the literal meaning of the words. A slightly deeper level of communicating focuses on data or content of verbalizations but uses prescriptive, exact, or denotative language. There is less room for misunderstanding the client's descriptions of experience. Often the focus in content is on times past and people or

Fig. 1-1

happenings distant. As the triangle or funnel constricts, communication occurs through emotions, nonverbal manifestations, situational deductions; at the point, communication consists of meanings or messages.

Frequently when clients arrive at the position of clarifying circumstances to the therapist, they have gained additional insight into acceptable solutions to their dilemmas, and counseling is terminated. When this is not the case, the application of some problem-solving method or intervention strategy is necessary.

In the case of a Freudian therapist, a Gestalt therapist, a rational-emotive therapist, or others, the method or strategy will be determined by therapist bias or preference. In responsive therapy the method or strategy is selected and applied in response to the particular problem(s) and the style of the client.

Later chapters will point out that most therapy approaches are "narrow-band" instruments; that is, they work best with certain kinds of clients and on certain types of problems. A therapist who is limited to one specialty must either force clients into acceptance of it, select clients who fit (this obviously happens in the case of very reputable therapists who draw certain types of clients), refer many clients who don't fit, or simply fail to do effective therapy.

Eclecticism, the process of selecting bits and pieces from many models and incorporating them into a personalized approach, is seen by many therapists as being preferable to the seemingly straitjacket approach of the specialist. Criticism of the eclectic approach centers on two premises. The first is that application of techniques outside their philosophical or theoretical context is improper and renders the techniques powerless. The second concern is that two or more techniques from different models applied simultaneously or in sequence to one client may work in opposing directions, effectively canceling each other.

Responsive therapy requires that the therapist be skilled in at least three different "specialities" so that each can be used philosophically and theoretically intact with those clients whose problems and styles fit the specialty.

There may be temptation to dismiss the responsive therapy viewpoint as just another way of being eclectic. With but very little concentrated attention and discriminative intent, it can be seen that not only are they different but the difference is sizable and the significance of the variation is profound.

Rather than being limited by one model, the responsive therapist has three that are representative of major families of therapy models. Rather than apply pieces of models out of context, the responsive therapist incorporates at least three intact models into a professional repertoire.

Here is an analogy that may help clarify the distinction. The specialty approach is like three musicians: one plays a classical selection very well, one plays a jazz number superbly, and one is polished in a country-western piece.

The eclectic approach is typified by one musician who knows a medley of themes from the classical selection, the jazz, and the country-western. The themes are artistically woven together, but the chord structures are absent or replaced by one of the artist's preference.

Responsive therapy resembles one musician who is skilled in the performance of a classical selection, a jazz number, and a country-western piece. The particular selection used at any given time results from the taste of the audience. Admittedly the analogy has some weaknesses, particularly in the implication of playing to an audience.

A different analogy compares counselors with artisans. Three are specialists: one with a hammer, a second with a screwdriver, and a third with a saw. Another artisan has invented a tool that has the balance of a hammer and the serrated edge of a saw, with each protrusion shaped like a screwdriver. The fifth artisan carries a toolbox and selects hammer, saw, or screwdriver depending on the task to be performed.

The use of analogy here is intended to clarify the philosophical differences among the approaches. It is not meant to depreciate any specific position; each has definite strengths and weaknesses.

In brief summary responsive therapy is an integrative approach which uses foundation skills in the initial stages to manage the therapy process while clarifying client style and circumstance. It then combines the awareness from the above process with application of an intervention program in a "theory-pure" context. Further elaboration of the theoretical foundations for responsive therapy is presented in the last chapter.

To complete the cognitive foundation necessary to progress into skill acquisition it will be helpful to give some attention to two complementary ways of viewing therapy.

ANALYZING THERAPY

Therapy can be described from several perspectives, one of which is the general sequence of experience. For example, the four stages in therapy are (a) ventilation, (b) clarification, (c) alteration, and (d) adaptation. Before accomplishing any change a client has to deal with a build-up of emotions. The process of expressing those emotions—talking, swearing, crying—is called ventilation. In and of itself ventilation usually is therapeutic. Most people feel better after having talked over or cried out their problem, whether to a relative, minister, bartender, or therapist.

Just ventilating does not solve the problem, and if nothing more is done, the emotions will build up again and a cycle of ventilation-buildup-ventilation is created. The second phase in therapy usually requires a skilled helper. This is the clarification phase. During this portion of therapy the helper causes clients to examine their unique, personal world through the process of communicating it to the helper. Often the clients see and describe themselves in new and insightful ways. This too is therapeutic, and in some models of counseling it is essentially the end of therapy. If the clients are seen as competent to solve problems but confused, then clarification is all that is needed.

In many circumstances, even though clients understand their problems, they need to be taught appropriate methods to solve the problems or alter the circumstances. This is the alteration phase. It is here that very specific methods with unique strengths can and should be selectively taught to clients in accord with their ability to understand and with the probability of their accepting and applying the solution.

For example, a client who is very unhappy, self-critical, and 100 pounds overweight establishes through the clarification process that he/she is using obesity as a defense or as an excuse to avoid the risk of failure in intimate social relationships and as a rebellion against an overdemanding, hard-to-satisfy parent. Simply knowing reasons for the condition may allow the client to decide to be different and may permit increased motivation to diet and lose the weight.

On the other hand, the client may not know how to lose the weight effectively, how to manage realistic self-appraisal, or how to find sources of positive personal validation. Teaching from the standpoint of a behavior modifier could be very useful in altering food consumption patterns. A Gestalt therapist could provide learning experiences in intrapersonal integration. Instruction in assertive techniques or social relations would facilitate establishment of a validating social environment.

The selection of the particular alteration plan or intervention strategy should be a result of the problem circumstances, client style, and client resources. Bibliotherapy would not typically be the prescribed method for a nonreader to learn about social graces. Methods for altering emotional responsiveness are not very efficient when applied to intellectual conflict or to self-defeating behavior.

Adaptation refers to getting used to the changes. It is the "refreezing" phase of the Lewinian system of change, which requires an unfreezing of old behavior, a change, and a refreezing of the new pattern (Bennis, Berlew, Schein, & Steele, 1973).

As a simple example, consider a habit-change problem such as losing weight. Unfreezing has to do with becoming aware of what pattern is causing the problem; i.e., what is the client doing to maintain an obese condition? Change is the process of losing weight. Where weight is perceived as the problem, crash or fad diets are often effective in removing the weight; often, however, the problem recurs. Where the eating pattern is perceived as the problem, the change process attempts to replace that pattern with one that permits loss of weight down to the preferred amount and then maintenance of the desired body weight across an indefinite period. Refreezing is the process of managing the new behavior long enough for it to become habituated.

Parallel examples can be generated for self-initiated emotional crises, self-defeating social conflicts, and virtually every other client complaint.

Refreezing could be described as a process for bringing new behavioral patterns under client control.

One system for analyzing therapy, then, describes the four general phases through which the process moves. A second perspective focuses on the skills that facilitate the therapeutic process. The acronym SITE was introduced earlier in reference to a pattern of skills used to initiate therapy, track the client's expressions to progressively deeper levels of meaning, and enhance the process.

In addition to its use as a model for structuring an analysis of what goes on in counseling, the SITE skills organization provides a sequence or an approach to teaching prospective counselors how to conduct therapy. It must be realized that the events in therapy vary greatly from client to client. There tends to be, however, a general pattern or sequence that is assisted by or directed by these SITE skills:

  I.   Initiating skills
       A.   Indirect lead
       B.   Paraphrase of content
       C.   Summary of content
 II.   Tracking skills
       A.   Paraphrase of message
            1.   Reflection of feelings
            2.   Formalization of nonverbal cues
            3.   Description of situation
       B.   Summary of messages
III.   Enhancing skills—general
       A.   Proper use of silence
       B.   Physical contact, touch
       C.   Pacing
       D.   Minimizing interrogation
       E.   Perception checking
       F.   Managing the process
 IV.   Enhancing skills—specific
       A.   Cognitive methods
       B.   Affective methods

C. Behavioral methods
    1. Symptom control
    2. Social skills

Initiating skills are those used to structure the beginning of the therapy process. They effectively say to the client, "Give me an increasingly accurate representation of your phenomenal space. You tell me how things are for you." This establishes the most productive therapeutic interaction, wherein the person with the most information (client) assists the other (counselor) to understand; the person with the most knowledge of communication and perceptual dynamics (counselor) helps the other (client) to increase awareness of self and circumstances.

Examples and elaboration of initiating skills will be given in chapter 2. For the time being, consider indirect leads to be counselor instructions to clients to "tell me about you." Content paraphrases and summaries are skillful rephrases of client verbalizations that verify reception by the counselor and move the process in the direction of more precision, accuracy, and denotative production.

Tracking skills, in essence, focus on what is meant, rather than on just what is said by the client. The phenomenal experience of clients is very complex and the means of communication so elaborate that an accurate representation with words is impossible. Tracking is a skillful and artistic process of monitoring verbal, nonverbal, feeling, and situational channels, combining the information received from all of them, and restating conclusions to the client in precise, insightful ways.

Examples and elaboration of tracking skills will be given in chapter 3. Until then, consider tracking skills as an accurate counselor statement of what would follow the phrase "What you really mean, or how it really looks, seems, feels is——."

General process enhancers do not occur in as tight a sequence as the other skills. They are employed selectively and depend very much on the client. Some, like proper use of silence, will occur frequently but may vary in intensity, length, or quality. Others, like perception checking, may be used infrequently or not at all. Their purpose is to keep the process moving, help work through rough spots, avoid unnecessary diversions, and improve efficiency. They will be explained in detail in chapter 4.

Specific process enhancers are therapy models or counseling theories which address particular client conditions in ways that produce maximal client progress toward specific outcomes. They are organized into three groups relative to focus: cognitive, affective, behavioral.

Cognitive methods are geared to remedy problems resulting from ignorance or confusion and the accompanying upsets and/or faulty decisions. Affective methods address resolution of emotional turmoil, particularly that which involves ambivalent or competing emotions, and self-acceptance/validation conflicts. Behavioral methods focus on symptom removal; that is, the change of responses that are self-defeating—including, but not limited to, things such as overeating, smoking, procrastination, delinquency, and enuresis.

Specific process enhancers are treated in chapters 5 through 8. An overview of many different models is presented to afford a very brief but broad conceptualization of the field of therapeutic models; then a representative approach from each of the groups—cognitive, affective, behavioral—will be described in greater detail.

Collectively, the SITE system is a means for moving efficiently toward the core of a client's concerns, homing in on the bull's-eye of the target or moving through the funnel from the surface and general dynamics at the funnel's lip to the specific and focused action at the spout, and for applying an appropriate strategy for resolution of problems.

The four general phases of the therapy process were described: ventilation, clarification, alteration, adaptation. This was followed by consideration of skills used to manage therapy: sequential initiating, tracking, and enhancing skills. A combination of the two analytic approaches will complete the cognitive foundation section.

During the ventilation phase, the objective is for the client to express pent-up emotions, primarily through talking. The initiating skills, which start the process and facilitate its orderly accomplishment, are most appropriate and effective for this phase. The general enhancing skills also are very helpful in this phase.

Tracking skills are central to the clarification phase. Obtaining a fairly objective awareness of what's happening, from the client's perspective, and of client's options for resolution requires the learning and processing of messages and the understanding of client situations. Once again, selective use of general process enhancers is necessary here.

The phase of alteration requires techniques that efficiently and effectively aid the client, from problem confrontation through problem resolution. Specific process enhancers, those focused, narrow-band methods, provide the means for coaching the client through the alteration phase.

There are no particular SITE skills associated with the adaptation phase. Certainly the tracking and general process enhancers will be useful here. The role of the therapist in adaptation is to provide continual monitoring, support, and reinforcement. It is a process of weaning the client slowly but surely away from reliance on the therapist. There is a similarity to moving from immobility and casting of a broken bone, to crutch, to walking cast, to final examination. Of course, availability for help in the event of a relapse is a part of the therapist's final phase responsibility.

Ultimately, psychotherapy is a very personal event that probably defies accurate description. Therapists or helpers can only describe, relate, or organize those things that seem consistently to promote or enhance change in the client. This book is an attempt to integrate the sequence of experience and that of procedures in a philosophically consistent manner, to describe the elements of a truly responsive therapy.

SUMMARY

There seems to be confusion and competition among various proponents of therapeutic methods as to which is truly effective. This is further confounded by untrained, nonprofessional people demonstrating therapeutic results in some relationships.

Studies and writings that emphasize the common elements or similarities in various kinds of therapy offer the possibility that contrasting theories are merely part of a larger whole, rather than distinct entities by themselves.

Effective therapists employ a set of skills that permit management of the therapeutic interaction in a way that enhances communication flow from the client without distortion or misdirection. This provides the most efficient access to the client's phenomenal space.

The set of common skills occurs quite naturally in a pattern for sequential initiating, tracking, and enhancing. Mastery of the SITE skills allows the therapist to identify client circumstances and style prior to selection and application of theory-specific interventions. Such an approach makes it possible to avoid the shortcomings in methods employed by both a rigid disciple and an atheoretical eclectic.

Therapy can be described by four stages: (a) ventilation, (b) clarification, (c) alteration, and (d) adaptation. It can be divided according to the dynamics of interaction as managed by the therapist, namely, the initiating or beginning phase, the tracking or understanding position, and those segments geared toward enhancement of the therapeutic interaction or enhancement of problem resolution. The two systems, stages and dynamics, can be combined for a more complete understanding of and training for therapy.

Understanding of the process and mastery of the skills provides a therapist with the tools to engage in truly responsive therapy.

Chapter 2

INITIATING THE COUNSELING PROCESS

Successful therapy can occur in a variety of places and under a wide range of circumstances. There are some guidelines, however, that provide increased probability of success when followed.

EXTERNAL ENVIRONMENT

The basic general principle concerning the physical environment for counseling is that nothing in the environment draws attention away from the therapeutic interaction. This means that (a) temperature should be moderate and comfortable; (b) furniture be soft but not too soft, impressive but not ostentatious; (c) noise be absent, or at least unintelligible; (d) lighting be soft but not too low; (e) interruptions be minimized, phone calls intercepted, entering of space by others prevented; (f) visual distractions be reduced or eliminated; (g) furnishings be arranged so as to reduce or remove differences in status or other barriers between therapist and client.

Internal Environment: Counselor

There is a parallel between external and internal environments in two ways: (a) therapy can be successful even with a competitive environment, and (b) it tends to go much better when distractions are limited or absent. The client deserves the full attention of the therapist; however, therapists are human and subject to all of the problems that entails. Illness, dissonant relationships, overextension of energy and means, professional considerations, and even occasional aversions to what they are doing and with whom impinge on counselors as readily as on anyone else. Rules for the therapist in this regard include the following:

1. Resolve personal problems outside the session.
2. Level with self and with the client relative to interpersonal factors affecting both of them; i.e., discuss frankly and openly anything that may have a negative effect on therapy.
3. Monitor self so that the client can be postponed, rescheduled, or referred at any time when the therapist is unable to perform effectively and professionally because of competing interests.

Internal Environment: Client

Almost by definition the internal state of the client is disturbed, confused, and self-defeating. One major reason for establishing a therapeutic relationship is the creation of an internal environment facilitative of productive change for the client. Creating such a relationship is one of the early and high-priority objectives in therapy. The skills employed by the counselor in the initial stages of the interview are critical in setting up a supportive and yet work-promoting relationship. Given the probability of internal client states that prohibit self-awareness or the ability to work on their problems, there is a necessity to alter those internal states. Studies of tension demonstrate that too much anxiety prevents effective learning, and too little tension also produces poor learning (Speilberger, 1966). To the extent that learning is a process of change and therapy is a special, change-promoting, learning experience, too high an emotional state or near absence of affect (emotionality) will inhibit or prevent therapeutic progress.

Ventilation, the talking out, swearing, crying-out behavior of a highly emotional client, is the natural process of reducing tension to a tolerable level. This process should be encouraged and allowed to run its course without much interruption. Frequently several sessions are necessary to accomplish adequate ventilation.

There are two problems in the ventilation process that require special attention and careful management. The first has to do with monitoring or pacing the amount and depth of ventilation. Many clients will give too much, too fast. This results in a feeling of vulnerability and embarrassment because the therapist, virtually a total stranger, knows too much. Conversely, if not enough ventilation occurs, the client may be disappointed or discouraged with therapy. Client dropout after the first session is frequently a result of too little or too much ventilation.

It is advisable to spend relatively little time in formally structuring the therapy interaction or in social niceties, so as to get into ventilation early. Scheduling a second session within a day or two is much better than extending the interview beyond an hour because the client is really into it.

The second problem relative to management of ventilation occurs at the transition between it and the phase of problem definition, processing, and resolution. Many times the feeling that accompanies proper and thorough ventilation is so satisfying that clients believe they are cured and therefore do not need to continue in therapy. One of the many paradoxes in counseling is that when the intense motivation to work has subsided, it is time for the most productive work. Counselors can facilitate the transition by formalizing awareness on the part of the client, such as "Now my energies are not required to merely hold myself together, I can use them to solve the problems that caused my pain"; or "Now I've taken care of the discomfort, what can be done to prevent its occurring again?"

Occasionally, clients will present no obvious need for ventilation, no highly emotional state. This may be because someone referred them at a time when they were not quite ready to do therapeutic work or because their emotional turmoil is so high and threatening that they have suppressed any emotional expression. In either event there appears to be too little affect (emotionality) to produce change.

Proceeding with initiating and tracking skills is the appropriate strategy for both high-affect and low-affect clients, although progress may be slow, with lots of repetition in the case of low-affect clients.

APPROACH

The proper and effective use of certain skills at the outset is critical to the establishment of proper structure and a therapeutic relationship. The counselor's objective is to communicate to the client the messages:

1. "You talk; I understand."
2. "You set the direction; I track."
3. "You provide the material; I control and direct the process."

Clients often are pretty much in the dark about how to be good clients in general and especially about how to be a good client for their particular therapist. Therapy is an interaction for which virtually no client receives training; the stereotypes from television and movies are distorted, and each therapist proceeds in an individualized way. The first task for the counselor, then, is to teach the process of therapy to the client.

There are several ways to go about initiating the client to therapy. Some therapists believe that it is advisable to spend much of the first session on social amenities and conversation to make the client comfortable. At some particular time a mutual awareness of getting down to work is experienced, and therapy begins.

There are several weak aspects to this procedure. The initial session is a model for subsequent sessions. Time invested in "nothing talk" in the first session, when duplicated in later sessions, becomes time wasted. Sometimes this can be avoided by making a transition in structure during the later sessions.

A more serious problem with starting by socializing is that the dynamics for social interaction run counter to those of good therapeutic communication. The client has been taught to see the therapist as a conversationalist and as someone who directs the content.

Perhaps a more efficient way to teach clients about therapy is to instruct them formally. The counselor describes how the client must disclose phenomenological experience, which the counselor will paraphrase, reflect, or process in various ways that will lead the client to increased awareness and problem-solving insight. Three major difficulties exist with this approach. First, clients do not often speak or understand therapy talk. Second, time spent in formalizing structure is time taken from therapy. Third, clients tend to expect the counselor to carry all of the subsequent interaction.

The preferred method for teaching structure is to use the initiating skills which permit teaching through doing. Effectively coaching clients into disclosure followed by understanding on the part of the therapist produces a feeling of relief for the client, both from the standpoint of getting through a new encounter smoothly and also getting into the purpose for the encounter, namely, therapy. The advantages of this approach include proper modeling for subsequent sessions, establishment of appropriate dynamics, and efficiency.

A slogan for beginning therapy with a new client might go something like "Don't beat around the bush; don't talk about it; just do it!"

INITIATING SKILLS

In order for therapy to be productive, clients must communicate their content in their individual style and in a sequence determined by them. The initiating skills called indirect leads, paraphrase of content, and summary of content are tools for establishing therapist control of the process and moving quickly into a working interaction where clients maintain control of content, style, and sequence.

Indirect Leads

Any counselor statement that conveys "tell me about your-self," "tell me more," or "give me a specific example" is an indirect lead. The exact words and type of indirect lead will vary with therapist, client, and sequence of dynamics.

The "tell me about yourself" type of indirect lead usually occurs at the beginning of therapy immediately following the brief social amenities. Following are some examples:

"Tell me about yourself."

"Share with me what's happening in your life."

"I need to get a feeling for who you are. Tell me some things about you."

"Give me some background on you (on what's concerning you now) (on what brought you to me)."

"In order for counseling to work, you need to talk, and I need to listen and understand; so talk about anything you would like to."

Often a client will request more structure by asking the therapist to be more specific; e.g., "What do you want me to talk about?" or "What do you want to know?"

This represents a critical point in establishing the dynamics of the interaction. Inherent in the question is a structure where the counselor asks questions and the client is in the position of control and can choose to give acceptable answers, pleasing answers, incomplete answers, misleading answers, or no answers at all. The therapist must struggle to ask questions that are pertinent to the client's "problem," which is a mystery until the client describes it, and then the therapist must somehow decipher what is truly going on from the answers selectively given by the client. If the counselor gives up control of the process at this time, the therapeutic interaction will probably deteriorate quickly into a "twenty questions" game or an interrogation. Only by studiously avoiding closed questions—the type that can be answered with yes, no, or a one- or two-word reply—can the therapist avoid the interrogation trap.

Although it is true that almost any type of interaction can be used to advantage by a seasoned therapist—even interrogation, strong confrontation, and insult—most successful therapists most of the time will avoid such tactics until a working relationship has been established.

So what can therapists do when a client asks, "What do you want to hear?" They have basically two choices of effective response. The first is to give initiative back to the client by saying something like

"You decide."
"Whatever is happening with you."
"I'm not sure, so just begin with whatever comes to mind."

A second tactic is to give a multiple-choice lead; e.g., "Oh, I don't know, maybe some background information like family history, where you're from, what you're doing now, relationships you have, concerns, frustrations . . ." Such a lead requires the client to make a choice and to divulge more of self than through response to a closed question. Chances are pretty good that the chosen topic will be important to the client and hence more useful to therapy than would a short reply to a closed question, which would at best satisfy a curiosity of the counselor.

Remember that the major purpose of early indirect leads is to get the process started properly. If successful, clients will expose or give hints of their agenda, establish a direction for the counselor to track, and give *process control* to the therapist.

The "tell me about yourself" type of indirect lead is useful at the beginning of subsequent sessions but usually takes on a slightly different quality; e.g.:

"Share with me where you're at now."
"What's happening today for you?"
"Fill me in on important feelings, thoughts, or happenings since last time."
"Bring me up to date."

Such leads have the effect of helping the counselor get into the proper frame of mind relative to the specific client, and more important, allowing the client to introduce new material or new perspectives. A very close follow-up on the previous session may prevent more important material from coming up and also denies the fact of therapeutic growth happening between sessions.

An indirect lead at the beginning of each session reaffirms the process dynamics of "You talk, I track" or "You work, I coach."

Occasionally during a session the client will pause or stop, presumably having satisfactorily explained him/herself but leaving the therapist hanging. It is here that the furthering response "tell me more" is appropriate. Some examples are:

> "Please expand on that a little."
> "Give me a few more details."
> "I'm not sure I understand. Tell me more."

The most powerful type of furthering response is "Give me an example." It is common for clients to share conclusions in semiknowledgeable, often psychological terms. "I've got a depression" or "It's like I'm not really in control" are a couple of examples. This is similar to a person telling a physician, "I've got appendicitis." The physician would be foolish to initiate an appendectomy without checking the experiences or complaints which led the patient to that conclusion. Similarly, by asking for specific examples therapists can understand more clearly what is actually happening to the client and ascertain the client's meaning of "depression" or "not in control" or whatever. This allows therapists to draw their own conclusions relative to the disruptive dynamics in the client's life.

Paraphrase of Content

Another skill that is helpful in initiating therapy and bridging into the tracking phase is paraphrase of content. It is a statement by the therapist of what the client just said. It is not exactly the same words, which would be simply parroting the client, but is usually the same content said more briefly with more precise, denotative words. It's the sort of thing you would say following the phrase "What you're saying is" or "What you're telling me is." Beginners may use such phrases preceding a paraphrase as a reminder of what they're doing; however, a really good para-phrase does not include them. Paraphrases of content are voiced in a matter-of-fact, declaratory way; they do *not* end with an up-ward inflection or question hook. If stated as a question, they be-come closed questions answered by yes or no, thus stopping the flow and inviting a change to an interrogative interaction.

Some examples of paraphrase of content are:

> *Client:* I don't know . . . sometimes I think I'm jinxed or something. Like this morning . . . my alarm clock didn't ring so I was late to work, and on the way I had a near accident, and my emo-tions were frazzled so when the boss men-tioned I was late, I told him to "stick it in his ear." Some days it just doesn't pay to care.
>
> *Counselor:* You experienced some bad events today, be-ginning with a nonfunctioning clock, all of which seemed to you to be outside your con-trol.
>
> *Client:* My spouse does some of the dumbest things . . . like mouthing off and scolding me for little inconsequential things. I really dislike that kind of treatment. But on the other hand, there are times when I wouldn't want to be married to any other person. I feel very fortu-nate to have the partnership and love. . . .
>
> *Counselor:* You find yourself both irritated and pleased by certain actions of your spouse.

The effect of successful paraphrase of content is threefold. First, it helps to establish an atmosphere of acceptance, warmth, and positive regard. It says, "I care about what you are trying to tell me." Second, it supports the structure of interaction by en-couraging the client to go further toward increased disclosure. Third, a good paraphrase of content moves the interaction from imprecise, connotative communication filled with excess and confusing meaning toward a more precise, denotative communi-cation that is less subject to misunderstanding.

Note should be taken that a good, useful paraphrase of content need not always be accurate or complete. It is merely an attempt on the part of therapists to disclose their awareness of the client's statement. A slightly incorrect paraphrase typically evokes an attempt on the part of the client to correct the misunderstanding, thus furthering the interaction. Also it should be recognized that early content may not be significant for anything except as a vehicle for ventilation or establishment of relationship. In other words, the importance is in the fact that something be said, more so than what it is that gets said. For example, clients may talk about vocational indecision, poor study habits, or some other socially acceptable or relatively insignificant topic to sort of test the water before getting down to an identity crisis, incestuous occurrence, contemplation of suicide, or other serious concern.

Paraphrases of content are more useful during the early stages of therapy as a follow-up to indirect leads. They will ordinarily give way to the more effective tracking techniques as soon as ventilation is well under way and the basic interactional process has been established.

Summary of Content

By the limiting nature of communication, information comes from the client in a linear, one-at-a-time fashion. The reality experienced by the client is not so simple and orderly. This being the case, it is helpful to both partners in therapy, client and counselor, occasionally to review what has been discussed. It is a highly unusual experience for a client to explain his/her circumstances in an orderly, meaningful fashion. More often than not, client output is similar to that of the preadolescent child relating the sequence of a movie or television show with frequent corrections in the form of "Oh, I forgot. Back before the train derailed . . ." Sometimes there will be several themes (problems, concerns) that are verbalized in shotgun fashion, with alternation back and forth among those themes.

Summaries of content permit counselors to review periodically, out loud, the major ideas in a sequence that makes sense to them. This provides for verification of content, allows both partners to look for patterns or recurring themes, and tends to pace the flow of information and analysis—picking up the pace when there are major gaps in the story and slowing it down when the informational output is too fast to assimilate.

The following is an example of summary of content:

Counselor: Let's see now. You've talked about three areas: your school years, which were sort of mixed up—with success in studying but not too much social success; your employment pattern of doing well in jobs where you worked alone and could control your activities but not so well when closely supervised; and your marriage and the tendency to like, love, appreciate your spouse when away from home and seeming inability to tolerate "interference" that comes when you're closely involved.

COUNSELOR PRESENCE

Earlier in the chapter there was a section on external environment and the principle that nothing in the environment should draw attention from the therapeutic interaction. The therapist is part of the client's external environment. There are counselor characteristics and actions that may run counter to effective therapy and some that are very enhancing.

Although it is probably foolish to advise prospective therapists to be something other than what they are, it is probably wise for them to consider emphasizing those parts of their nature and style that will enhance their success. Extremes of dress, jewelry, hair style, cologne, and language (highbrow or street talk) tend toward distraction of clients. The adjectives describing environment also can be applied to counselor appearance and manner: moderate and comfortable, impressive but not ostentatious. An air of competence and of cautious optimism is helpful; arrogance or reference to self is counterproductive.

There are some types of behavior that can be consciously cultivated, the mastery of which is very helpful in therapy. A smile as recognition of the value of a client, even if it's the beginning of the sixth consecutive interview on a given day, goes a long way toward starting things off right.

Variation in the form and intonation of the beginning indirect lead may mean the difference between communicating to clients "I'm really interested in you" and "Ho hum. We might as well get started." For the therapist beginnings may be repetitious and mundane. It needs to be remembered that clients haven't heard the same indirect lead before or often, and each client deserves the therapist's best shot.

Nonverbal cues like posture, eye contact, and nod of head can signal counselor attentiveness or lack thereof. Generally an erect yet comfortable posture with relatively continual eye contact and an occasional nod of the head produces both the perception and the experience of attentive listening. These, combined with accurate paraphrases, communicate effective hearing. Of course, consistency or congruence between nonverbal cues and the words spoken is necessary to demonstrate genuineness.

Some therapists may successfully violate some of these principles, but in general they form a standard for counselor presence.

FUNNEL ANALOGY

The communication process in the initiating and tracking phases of counseling can be likened to a funnel (see Figure 1-1). Content exists primarily in the plane crossing the lip or top portion of the funnel. Immediately below the content level are underlying messages and feelings. At or near the spout or bottom of the funnel is the point of greatest dynamics where messages, themes, and situational clues establish the problem or concern or self-defeating characteristic of the client's life and style that creates the need for therapy.

Almost from birth people are taught to talk around subjects, to obscure feelings, to be tactful—in short, to be good conversationalists. Not that there is anything wrong with social grace and propriety as guides to social interaction, but the rules of good communication often run counter to those of good conversation.

After years of verbal production and exchange about relatively superficial topics or about deeper topics in careful conversational language, people tend to begin and to remain at a fairly shallow level. This level, primarily made up of talk about things (content) is represented by the top of the funnel (Figure 2-1).

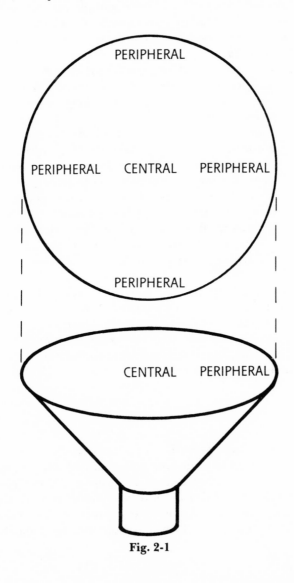

Fig. 2-1

The content can be thought of as central, or more important to clients, with progressively less significant material being located toward the periphery.

Initiating skills invite clients to share content with no restrictions on where they begin. A shy or threatened client may choose to share content that is very peripheral and very safe. The more assured or more motivated client can start with central content. Subsequent therapist involvement in processing content tends to elaborate the field and identify central content.

Probably more important than what is talked about are the dynamics of "client talks, counselor listens." This allows the person who knows most about the client to manage content and the therapist to manage the process.

Much the same as with a funnel, where all material at the top flows down through the body and out of the spout, all content at the top is related to or transformed into messages and themes. It is not sufficient to work only with content, because the more important dynamics are sometimes disguised or so embedded in the content that they are difficult to discern. Nor is it necessary to explore all possible content. Once some major messages and themes are known, the processing of them leads more rapidly and efficiently toward problem definition and resolution.

Indirect leads permit clients to begin where they are most comfortable. Paraphrases and summaries of content encourage and facilitate movement toward central content.

Additional techniques are required to get below the content level. They will be described in chapter 3, and more will be said about the funnel.

SUMMARY

Although therapy can happen under many conditions, some are more efficient or productive than others. A supportive external environment that does not draw attention away from therapy is helpful. Likewise, internal counselor and client environments can facilitate or impede progress. The counselor needs to monitor him/herself and also help the client through ventilation and/or other experiences to create the most productive internal environment.

The counseling interaction should be established early in therapy and controlled by the counselor. The most efficient interaction requires the client to produce and the counselor to understand. Skills for initiating this process are indirect leads, paraphrase of content, and summary of content.

Therapeutic communication is likened to a funnel, with content at the top, messages and themes in the middle, problem dynamics and personal style at the spout. The initiating skills of indirect leads, paraphrase of content, and summary of content serve to establish the proper interaction and allow clients to begin with content they are relatively comfortable with and move systematically toward more central content.

EXERCISES

This portion of the book will provide two sections of exercises, one very simple and one more difficult. Each section will be followed by answers and examples for that section.

Simple Exercises
Comparison responses begin on page 47.

   I.   Indirect leads (the basic form for indirect leads was "tell me about yourself.")
        A.   Write as many variations of the "tell me" portion as you can, e.g., "Explain to me——."
        B.   Write as many variations of the "about yourself" portion as you can; e.g., "what is happening in your life."
        C.   Label the following statements as indirect leads or other. Remember that indirect leads do not telegraph or advertise the expected response, neither can they be answered in a one- or two-word reply.
             1.   Share with me what you are feeling.
             2.   Give me your ideas on money management.
             3.   How are you today?
             4.   Can you tell me what you are feeling now?

5. How would you go about solving this problem?
6. Is there more than one possible solution?
7. Could you share with me the events leading up to your breakdown?
8. Of course you would agree with Dr. Smith.
9. We certainly have had nice weather this week.
10. You know, therapists are terribly underpaid.
11. Describe for me what it is like being you.
12. What is the most exciting thing that ever happened to you?
13. Tell me more about your reaction.
14. Sometimes I get really angry too.
15. What, in your estimate, are the critical factors in a good relationship?

II. Paraphrase of content
   A. Write a paraphrase of content for the following:
      1. You really ought to be more careful of what you say. That last remark was not correct, and I find it offensive.
      2. I really thought that I had resolved my bad feelings about the boating accident, but then, after all these years, they discovered the boats on the bottom of the lake. It seems like raising the wreckage is also raising all those terrible feelings too.
      3. School is certainly a challenge for me. Even though I have a 2.0 grade average, almost all of the programs I want to pursue require higher grades.
      4. Medicine just doesn't seem to be right for me. I'm doing okay in all my courses, but I just can't get excited about being a doctor. Maybe I should "shop around" for another career.
      5. He is the perfect husband—so considerate and helpful. He doesn't seem to be jealous of my success and really pulls his share of our "common duties." The only thing I don't like is his snoring. You can't believe how annoying that is.

B. For each of the same five statements as in II-A, select the paraphrase of content from the four responses, and then compare it to your paraphrase of content for the same item.

1. You really ought to be more careful of what you say. That last remark was not correct, and I find it offensive.

    (a) Describe for me your perception of what I said and how it offended you.

    (b) I didn't mean to hurt your feelings, and I'm sorry if my statement was inaccurate.

    (c) What I said is not true and bothers you; I need to pay more attention to what I say.

    (d) Was it my reference to your illegitimate birth that offended you?

2. I really thought that I had resolved my bad feelings about the boating accident, but then, after all these years, they discovered the boats on the bottom of the lake. It seems like raising the wreckage is also raising all those terrible feelings too.

    (a) People who dredge up the past really do not consider the effects it may have on others.

    (b) Somehow the discovery and retrieval of the boats are creating a bad emotional experience for you, even though you thought you had adjusted to the accident.

    (c) Boats are dangerous, especially when driven at high speeds and under conditions of poor visibility. We need better regulation of boats and boaters.

    (d) You'd think that an adult like you would have better control over emotions and not let a little thing like wreckage set you off again.

3. School is certainly a challenge for me. Even though I have a 2.0 grade average, almost all of the programs I want to pursue require higher grades.

(a) You are having a struggle at school because your most desired programs require grades higher than you have been getting.

(b) School is supposed to be a challenge. If you already knew it, you wouldn't have to go to school.

(c) Since 2.0 is defined as average, although everybody knows it's not, it is wrong for any program to set higher entrance requirements.

(d) Why don't you drop out and go to work for your uncle?

4. Medicine just doesn't seem to be right for me. I'm doing okay in all my courses, but I just can't get excited about being a doctor. Maybe I should "shop around" for another career.

(a) The medicine you're taking is making you sick so you wonder if your doctor is really qualified.

(b) You should stick with it anyway because even bad doctors make lots of money.

(c) Where is it written that you have to enjoy your job?

(d) Even though you are succeeding, your lack of enthusiasm for a career in medicine is causing you to consider other alternatives.

5. He is the perfect husband—so considerate and helpful. He doesn't seem to be jealous of my success and really pulls his share of our "common duties." The only thing I don't like is his snoring. You can't believe how annoying that is.

(a) Except for his snoring, which bothers you a great deal, you judge your husband to be really okay.

(b) Why don't you sleep in another room?

(c) What a petty thing to say. I'm sure he can't help it.

(d) You've got nothing to complain about. My

husband has stinky feet, and he picks his nose!

III. Summary of content

Assume that statements 2, 4, and 5 from the previous exercise were said by the same person, and write a summary of content.

Comparison Responses

I. Indirect leads
   A. Variations of the "tell me" portion.
      1. Share with me ____.
      2. Describe for me ____.
      3. How does ____ appear to you?
      4. Give me an example of ____.
      5. How is it to ____?
      6. What are your thoughts on ____?
      7. How would you ____?
      8. Fill me in on ____.
      9. Bring me up to date concerning ____.
      10. Talk to me about ____.
      11. Provide me with ____.
   B. Variations of the "about yourself" portion.
      1. what it's like being you.
      2. events in your life.
      3. two or three greatest concerns or challenges.
      4. events leading up to your coming here.
      5. how you see yourself; your circumstances; your space.
      6. what's going on in your life now.
      7. your thoughts on ____.
      8. what alternatives you have considered.
      9. background information.
      10. something about you.
      11. how you'd like it to be.
   C. Labels for counselor statements.
      1. Share with me what you are feeling.
         Indirect lead: technically correct, good lead.
      2. Give me your ideas on money management.

Indirect lead: technically correct, focuses on cognitive data about a prescribed topic but does not telegraph intended response.

3. How are you today?
   Other: A standard conversational ritual that telegraphs expected response.

4. Can you tell me what you are feeling now?
   Other (although it may produce similar results to an indirect lead): technically incorrect—"Can you" sets up a potential yes or no response. Also the focus on feelings *now* is quite narrow and will likely set up an interrogational structure.

5. How would you go about solving this problem?
   Indirect lead: technically correct, useful lead.

6. Is there more than one possible solution?
   Other: yes/no response.

7. Could you share with me the events leading up to your breakdown?
   Other: like No. 4, technically incorrect leading to yes/no answer. Would be very good without the words "Could you."

8. Of course you would agree with Dr. Smith.
   Other: telegraphs intended response.

9. We certainly had nice weather this week.
   Other: chitchat.

10. You know, therapists are terribly underpaid.
    Other: irrelevant.

11. Describe for me what it is like being you.
    Indirect lead: technically correct, broad, excellent lead.

12. What is the most exciting thing that ever happened to you?
    Other: too focused, can be answered with one or few words.

13. Tell me about your reaction.
    Indirect lead: technically correct, furthering response.

14. Sometimes I get really angry too.
    Other: irrelevant.

15. What, in your estimate, are the critical factors in a good relationship?
Indirect lead: like No. 2, cognitively oriented, good lead.

II. Paraphrase of content
   A. You can compare your responses to those in section II-B as well as considering the following analyses of the statements (see page 45). A complete paraphrase would include the folllowing:
      1. Prescription to be more careful; challenge to correctness of statement; the taking of offense to it.
      2. Assumption that feelings were resolved; the event: discovery and raising of wreckage; emotional reaction.
      3. School is difficult; desired programs require more than I've got (a 2.0 gpa).
      4. Concern about career choice; doing okay *but*; lack of enthusiasm or excitement; shop around.
      5. Husband is perfect (examples are not necessary but okay) *except* he snores; his snoring is annoying.
   B. Keyed responses for multiple-choice items:
      1. (c); 2. (b); 3. (a); 4. (d); 5. (a).

III. Summary of content
   A combination of statements 2, 4, and 5 from II: "You've related information about three areas—your emotional response to the discovery and raising of the boat wreckage, the concern about your choice of medicine when you have limited enthusiasm for it, and your near-perfect husband whose snoring is a problem for you."

Exercises of a More Difficult Nature
Comparison responses begin on page 54.

I. Indirect leads
   Basically, any lead that produces more than a yes, no, or a one- or two-word reply is an indirect lead; however, there are varying degrees of effectiveness. Generally, the more

effective leads are those that maximize breadth; i.e., those that give the client the most latitude or freedom to choose content. The model, "Tell me about you," is a good reference for structuring indirect leads. Do the following exercises, but recognize that you will probably not perform perfectly. Look at this as more of a learning exercise than a test.

A. You are a counselor who has just received a new client into your office. You have finished the brief social amenities and are ready to go to work. Write three different indirect leads for initiating the process.

B. This is the beginning of the fourth session with your client. Write three indirect leads for getting this session under way.

C. Label the following statements direct or indirect and analyze each regarding probable effectiveness.
    1. Tell me about yourself.
    2. Why did you do that?
    3. Do you feel happy?
    4. How do you feel now?
    5. How much do you weigh?
    6. What is that like for you?
    7. Tell me about your fear.
    8. Tell me more about that.
    9. Did you go to the party last night?
    10. I would like to hear you elaborate on that.
    11. Please tell me why you are here.
    12. How is it going?
    13. Tell me about Spain.
    14. Share with me your ideas on women's sports.
    15. Give me some idea of how you go about doing that.

II. Paraphrase of content
    A. Write a paraphrase of content for the following:
        1. I'm about $400 in debt. My car insurance is being increased because of that accident. Tuition is overdue, and the bank has been trying to contact me about being overdrawn. I really hate to go to

my father for help. He will bail me out, but it makes me feel like a failure.

2. During my trip to Mexico I met the neatest guy. We really hit it off well. Never have I felt so strongly for someone, nor given so freely and totally. I know I can't pursue the relationship because of all the problems involved. But how can I tell my fiancé; and how can I accept him when, comparatively, he seems so dull and ordinary?

3. Just because they are getting a divorce is no reason for them to hassle me. It's almost like they are fighting each other through me. I love them both and don't want to take sides. How can such wonderful people be so totally childish?

4. What's the big deal about being thirty-three years old and not married? I know lots of unmarried women, and they seem perfectly happy, but the way people talk, you'd think I'm some kind of freak or lesbian or something!

5. I want to be an auto mechanic, but at every school I go to I get teased so badly about being a woman that I end up quitting. Should I change my goal?

6. My sister smokes pot. She is only fifteen. I'm afraid that she's on the wrong path, but she retorts that her peers' approval is more important to her than mine.

B. For the following statement, select the best paraphrase of content from the four responses. Compare your choice with your own paraphrase from II-A; then check the key in the response comparison section.

1. I'm about $400 in debt. My car insurance is being increased because of that accident. Tuition is overdue, and the bank has been trying to contact me about being overdrawn. I really hate to go to my father for help. He will bail me out, but it makes me feel like a failure.

    (a)   It's really not fair for insurance companies to increase your premium just because you had an accident.

    (b)   It seems like problems come in bunches. You have a debt, more insurance to pay, a tuition bill, and no money in the bank.

    (c)   You have several financial problems—a $400 debt, increase in insurance, tuition overdue, and bank account overdrawn. The only solution you can see is to have your father help, but doing so will cause you some bad feelings about yourself.

    (d)   It's really bad to be dependent on your father. Although he has enough money to bail you out, you'd really like to prove that you can handle things yourself.

2.   During my trip to Mexico I met the neatest guy. We really hit it off well. Never have I felt so strongly for someone, nor given so freely and totally. I know I can't pursue the relationship because of all the problems involved, but how can I tell my fiancé; and how can I accept him when, comparatively, he seems so dull and ordinary?

    (a)   You fell in love with a guy in Mexico, but somehow you can't follow through on that relationship. You're left with a fiancé to whom you've made some promises that will be hard to keep since you prefer the other man.

    (b)   You let yourself get hooked on a vacation romance, and now you're paying the price.

    (c)   Your dishonesty and deceitfulness in not being true to your fiancé are now making it difficult to be happy with him.

    (d)   You are sorry for not being true to your fiancé and are having a hard time confessing to him, especially since now he seems so boring.

3.   Just because they are getting a divorce is no rea-

son for them to hassle me. It's almost like they are fighting each other through me. I love them both and don't want to take sides. How can such wonderful people be so totally childish?

(a) I wish they'd mind their own business and leave me alone.

(b) Your parents are being childish and using or abusing you in their divorce struggle. You love them both so you don't want to be seen as taking sides.

(c) It's so hard for you to see your parents breaking up that you just want to be left alone.

(d) People who are going to get divorced shouldn't have children.

4. What's the big deal about being thirty-three years old and not married? I know lots of unmarried women, and they seem perfectly happy, but the way people talk, you'd think I'm some kind of freak or lesbian or something!

(a) It's nobody's business whether or not you're married.

(b) Time is running out for you. You're really an old maid and don't want to face up to it.

(c) You're afraid that your sexual preference is confused and that you are a latent homosexual.

(d) Being thirty-three and unmarried is no cause for concern. You know some women that old who appear to be happy and normal.

5. I want to be an auto mechanic, but at every school I go to, I get teased so badly about being a woman that I end up quitting. Should I change my goal?

(a) You have been teased about wanting to be an auto mechanic so much that you have quit several training programs and are wondering about changing your goal.

        (b) You don't want to be a mechanic badly enough to put up with the teasing.

        (c) Equality in job opportunities is just a dream and won't ever happen.

        (d) There are times you'd really rather be a man.

6. My sister smokes pot. She is only fifteen. I'm afraid that she's on the wrong path, but she retorts that her peers' approval is more important to her than mine.

        (a) It makes you angry when your little sister doesn't do what you say.

        (b) Your sister's friends are leading her astray, and you think she should find some new friends.

        (c) You are afraid that your sister is doing wrong by smoking pot, but you can't do much about it because the influence of her peers is stronger than yours.

        (d) If pot were legalized, you would have no reason to be concerned about your sister's behavior.

III. Summary of content

Assume that the six client statements in II-A were made by the same client in the same session and write a summary of content.

Comparison Responses

I. Indirect leads

  A. New client

    1. Tell me about yourself.

    2. Share with me how you see yourself and your circumstances.

    3. Say something about yourself so I can get to know you a little better.

    4. Describe for me the events leading up to your coming to see me.

    5. What's it like being you?

      6. Talk to me about what's going on in your life now.

B. Continuing client
    1. Fill me in on what's happened since last time.
    2. How do you see things today?
    3. Share with me your thoughts about ____
    4. What's happening with you now?
    5. What's happened since we talked last?
    6. I'd like you to begin talking about what's important to you now.

C. Label and analyze
    1. Indirect, a good and very open lead.
    2. Indirect, not very good because of the word *why*. That particular word tends to evoke defensiveness.
    3. Direct
    4. Direct, weak because it forces a person to stop feeling long enough to think about it and because it can be answered in one word.
    5. Direct
    6. Indirect, basically a good lead. It does focus on a particular statement, thereby directing attention, but it's open enough to keep the client active.
    7. Indirect, a good lead, focused.
    8. Indirect, a good lead, a furthering response.
    9. Direct
   10. Indirect, okay, another furthering response.
   11. Indirect, not very good. Includes "why" and directs attention toward the problem and away from the person.
   12. Direct, terrible as an initiating lead because it is a social convention and not a request for communication.
   13. Indirect, a little weak because it directs attention away from the client and toward ideas or experiences relating to Spain.
   14. Indirect, weak because client is not free to choose the topic.

15. Indirect, weak because it focuses on a process; may be okay as a furthering response.

Note: Items 13, 14, and 15 are not necessarily bad leads. They do not permit the client to generate ideas that will communicate some style and data. Such leads may be helpful for a client who is uncomfortable with or resistant to counseling.

II. Paraphrase of content
   A. You can compare your responses to those in II-B of the exercises as well as considering the following analyses of the statements:
   1. In debt; insurance being increased; tuition overdue; bank account overdrawn; father can help, *but* I'll feel bad about myself.
   2. Relationship with guy in Mexico; can't pursue it; having difficulty telling fiancé, and hard to accept him because he's dull in comparison to other man.
   3. Parents are getting divorced, acting childish, fighting through me; I love them both; I don't want to take sides.
   4. Thirty-three years old and unmarried; concern about self; others in same situation seem okay.
   5. Want to be auto mechanic; quit several schools because of teasing; wondering about changing goals.
   6. Young sister smokes pot; influenced by peers; I judge behavior to be wrong, *but* my influence is not strong enough.
   B. Selection of best paraphrases of content. Although more than one of the alternative responses for each situation may be acceptable and therapeutic, only the keyed responses are paraphrases of content.
   1. (c); 2. (a); 3. (b); 4. (d); 5. (a); 6. (c).
   Remember that a paraphrase of content does not add or subtract appreciably from what literally was said.

III. Summary of content
      The order is not necessarily significant, but each area of
      concern should be paraphrased along with most of its ac-
      companying content. Compare your summary with this
      one:
         "You've expressed concern in six areas. There is the
      problem of being caught in the middle of your parent's di-
      vorce and not knowing how to maintain a neutral position;
      your Mexican vacation left you with the conflict of not
      knowing how to deal with a less-than-satisfactory fiancé
      when compared to the relationship you enjoyed in Mexico.
      Money is a problem in that you may have to have your fa-
      ther help you, which makes you feel like a failure, but the
      $400 debt, auto insurance, tuition debt, and bank prob-
      lems require some action; schooling is an issue, particu-
      larly since you're experiencing some difficulty over your
      age and marital status; and your little sister has you wor-
      ried in regard to her pot smoking and peer pressure."

Chapter 3

TRACKING SKILLS

In chapter 1 reference was made to the fact that progress beyond ventilation and through clarification, or movement in the funnel from surface to depth, usually requires assistance from a skilled helper. The skills most essential to this movement are referred to as tracking skills.

An analogy is inherent in such a label. Picture someone wandering through a dense forest, not sure of destination, confused as to how he/she got to the present location, doubtful of the ability to escape from the dilemma. Picture yourself as a competent scout, tracker, or explorer who knows the signs that show an earlier passage of a person and who is wise in the ways of survival within and navigation through the forest.

Your task is to find the lost traveler, provide reassurance of basic "OK-ness," develop a trusting relationship so you will be permitted to be a guide, determine precisely the desired destination, and help the person do what is necessary to get there. Note here that your task is not to get there *for* the person or to carry the traveler on your back—for to do so may cause you both to perish—but rather to teach or coach your charge into making the appropriate and necessary steps as a responsible individual.

The first step is to find the lost traveler. You read many signs—crushed grass, broken twigs, remains of campfires, discarded items, footprints, and the like. After a time you notice patterns of behavior that allow you to move ahead more quickly. You put yourself in the situation of the lost traveler, as nearly as you can imagine it, and say to yourself, "What would I do next?" Your conclusions from such imagining allow you to make some shortcuts, some of which are in error but most of which are accurate because of your skill and awareness from similar experiences in the past.

Your task would be easier if the traveler remained in one place or behaved in a consistent, meaningful pattern; however, even as you are gaining an understanding of one day's wandering, the traveler is moving ahead.

Eventually you overtake the wanderer, who immediately expresses a lot of emotion and eventually tells you how good it feels to have another person around. Of course the problem is not resolved until the person can communicate an intended destination and can accept your guidance out of the predicament.

Focus for a moment on the tracking. You had to be simultaneously alert for clues in many forms; you had to see the obvious—the footprints, the discarded items—and not so obvious—the crushed grass, the bent twigs. You had to imagine the emotional state of the wanderer and compute its effect within your awareness of the total situation. Only through having practiced such a complex process were you able to perform your task successfully.

Therapeutic tracking is very similar to finding lost travelers in the woods. Clients are lost, in that they have limited perception of where they are, how they got there, and how to get out of the predicament they are in. Their emotional state contributes to narrowed perception and the probability of self-defeating responses.

The task of the therapist is to follow client movement through client phenomenal space (life space or the total of perceived forces, people, or events having influence on the client at present). Since there are innumerable possible dynamics for any given person, the therapist's best or most efficient approach is to follow (track) the client through that space. Phenomenal tracking is done by relying on clients for evidence of where they are, what it's like being there, and what resources they have for progressing.

Instead of the obvious footprints and discarded items of the forest the counselor sees or hears obvious clues—the content of client verbalizations, tears, smiles, gestures—that accumulate to present a general idea of client experience and condition. The obvious clues are usually not enough to really know client phenomenal space, for when clients can describe their condition accurately and insightfully, they very frequently see solutions and adapt without therapeutic help.

Seasoned counselors look for the not-so-obvious clues to add to their awareness of client conditions. The crushed grass and bent twigs of therapy are things such as tension in muscles, speed variations in talk, contradictions between verbal content and body cues, and qualifiers such as "basically" or "but."

From experience, therapists often hear and process what is not said—the gaps in story, or "reading between the lines." Just as certain conditions of wilderness and lost travelers produce predictable actions on the part of the traveler, so do certain circumstances produce similar experiences or conditions for clients. Therapists, on recognizing some consistency in clues, can then make gentle inferences into undisclosed areas; for example, although no two people have identical experiences at the death of a loved one, there are enough similarities to guide therapeutic work.

Consider an analogy different from the lost traveler in the wilderness. The process of communicating through an advanced art form is an extremely complex and difficult process, unless thoroughly practiced. Take a musical selection for example. Really to understand and appreciate it, more than a superficial listening experience is necessary. One clue or message may be offered by the most prominent melodic line, another by a secondary theme, still another by a countermelody. The structure or chords supporting the melodies provides another message; the sequence of chords and their degree of adherence to or variation from a standard or predictable pattern tell a little more. The key structure, uniquely chosen for this selection, adds information. The particular instruments or voices give special meaning. Even more can be "heard" from the selection if you know something about the composer—personality and physical and emotional environment in which the composer lived. All of the data, experienced as a complex whole, provides a more nearly accurate communication between two people. Such a skill of being able to listen to or monitor several channels simultaneously, channels within the music and channels within yourself, is difficult to master but tremendously gratifying.

Therapy, like the musical experience, is aided by the counselor's being able simultaneously to hear content, see nonverbal cues, process similarities of present client condition with knowledge of normal or typical responses, read between the lines, tune in to emotional status, and synthesize all of these data into an accurate comprehension of client messages.

As you can see readily, wilderness tracking and accomplished artistic appreciation share some dynamic similarities to the process and experience of conducting therapy. Their description rolls easily off the pen; their mastery is considerably more difficult. Particularly is this so in making the transition from adequately processing content, which comes through skillful use of the initiating skills, to tracking clients into a relatively complete understanding of just what is happening.

Many students experience a leveling off or a plateau of pretty good content work but quite poor facility in hearing and processing messages. Perhaps like the shift from letter-by-letter typing to the typing of words or phrases, there seems to be a quantum leap as the effects of multiple processing replace the more limited focus on content alone.

DOWN THE FUNNEL

As described earlier, a well-initiated counseling interview invites the client to expose content that has some personal meaning or significance. Without help to proceed toward more depth the client will probably talk in content circles, periodically covering data that already have been discussed. Within the content of the superficial plane at the top of the funnel and parallel or simultaneous to it are "footprints, crushed grass, and bent twigs" that provide clues to a deeper meaning.

It may be helpful to differentiate verbiage from message. Not always do words efficiently convey meaning; it is possible to talk at length and yet say very little. Conversely, it is possible to utter few or no words and still communicate strong meaning. The words are verbiage; the meaning is message.

Sometimes words (verbiage) carry little or no indication of the intended meaning. The social convention of "Hello! How are you?" "I'm fine, thank you. How are you?" is an example of the use of words to conduct a social transaction that typically ignores the content of the words. Seldom does the initiator want to know the condition of the other person, and many times a positive reply is given even when the personal condition is far from "fine."

Words can be used in a very precise, dictionary-like manner. In these cases verbiage and message are closely related. Such use of words is called denotative language. Scientific reports rely on carefully used, definitive terms. In contrast, casual conversation often includes very imprecise words called connotative language. Slang and sarcasm often rely on vagueness of meaning for their effect.

An example of less precise use of words followed by denotative phrasing is this exchange between Sam and Harriet in their discussion of euthanasia.

> Sam: I sort of favor it. Not the intentional doing in of someone just because they're way over on the downhill side, but like when they're hooked up to all them machines and stuff and their lights are entirely out upstairs, I see nothing at all wrong with pulling the plug on them.
>
> Harriet: There are some cases where you favor the intentional termination of life. One example is the person who is brain-dead but being maintained by mechanical means. You would advocate turning off the life-support system in this case.

The reply by Harriet is a paraphrase of content, wherein she moved from a connotative statement by the client to a more precise, denotative version. Such a process is relatively easy to see in expressions of opinion or content interactions. It is more difficult when emotions, attitudes, past behavior, motives, and other variables are involved. In such cases, multiple-channel monitoring techniques are required, and the focus is on what was meant (meaning) rather than only on what was said (verbiage).

In multiple-channel monitoring, the words themselves form only one channel; the context of the verbal structure is a second channel. Another context, that of the environment in which words are shared, presents qualitative influences on messages. Nonverbal cues occur in yet another channel. The internal reactions of the therapist and the ability to conceptualize the client's words and other cues provide additional qualitative aspects of the communication process (see Figure 3-1).

This is all further complicated by client production coming word by word, action by action in a linear fashion. Even though 2 or 3 or 10 or 20 things may be happening to a client, only one word can be given at a time. One thing may be described systematically and thoroughly or not very well; several things may be

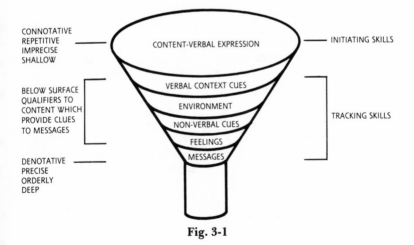

Fig. 3-1

juxtaposed or mixed together. The therapist must remember words, impressions, feelings, and observations in a continually active, kaleidoscopic mixture, scanning constantly for patterns and matching them against previous experiences and perceptions.

The understanding of client circumstances requires moving from the content level of client talk down through feelings and behavioral cues and situational occurrences to an awareness of and agreement on messages—what is really meant, what is really happening. The statement of this counselor awareness back to the client is called a paraphrase of message.

PARAPHRASE OF MESSAGE

The key to good therapy in the clarification phase is the skill of the therapist in "hearing" messages from the multiple-channel monitoring and then relating them back to the client in relatively simple, straightforward, denotative language. When confronted with an accurate translation of their confusing attempts at understanding and communicating their predicament, clients validate the accuracy of the therapist's paraphrase and simultaneously achieve personal insight.

Paraphrasing messages consists then of processing the complex inputs from the client and giving them back in a more precise form. It might well be preceded by the *silent* phrase "What I understand your predicament to be is . . ." or "The message I'm hearing is . . ." or "What you really mean to say is . . ."

The following are some examples of paraphrased messages:

> "You want very much to be successful, but can't quite bring yourself to try for fear of failure."
> "While it's hard to admit it out loud, you really dislike your mother and are angry at her for the way she treated you."

A paraphrase of message may be derived from a reprocessing of content, such as is done in variations of summarizing content. It may occur as a result of some emotional manifestation from the client. Sometimes a nonverbal cue will prompt a message paraphrase. It can come as a result of any of these events singularly; more often it results from a combination of several or all.

Although it is possible for a practiced professional to go directly from client response in any of the channels, usually the data from each channel is processed in some way and reflected back to the client. The processing of these channels will be described in the following sections on structure of content (including key words or "traffic signs"), reflection of feeling, formalization of nonverbal cues, and description of situation. Skill in each of these areas separately will contribute to increasing clients' awareness of their circumstances, but the strength from each is multiplied in combination with the others to refine and increase the power of paraphrases of messages.

STRUCTURE OF CONTENT

The process of paraphrasing content in more explicit, denotative language than used by the client has the effect of clarifying what was said. A further clarification and a major beginning of tracking comes from hearing and reflecting the structure of client verbiage.

Following an indirect lead by the therapist, clients generally proceed in one of two ways. The first, and most frequent, is to give a "thesis statement" very much like the way a good paragraph is written. This statement is a conclusion drawn from data in client phenomenal space that has yet to be disclosed. It may be a kind of diagnosis; e.g., "I think maybe I'm a little too compulsive" or "I've really been depressed lately." Sometimes it refers to the present state of mind; e.g., "I'm not really clear on this, but . . ." Emotional status can be signaled by the initial statement; e.g., "This has me very concerned" or "[I'm afraid to disclose this because] People might think I'm a little strange."

The topic statement made by clients is very helpful in assessing how they organize their perceptions of their reality. As for accuracy, that must be determined by subsequent information. It's the same idea presented earlier that physicians would be foolish to operate on patients' self-diagnoses; likewise, therapists should draw their own conclusions after getting considerable information and insight. Sometimes the first statement is not awfully significant, but usually it is very helpful and therefore important to be remembered by the therapist.

When clients begin with topic statements, they usually follow with elaboration or examples. "I'm not really sure, but last week when I . . ." or "I've been depressed lately. I just can't get enthused about anything. Even special attention from my family seems remote, like there is a thick window between us."

One structure for content, then, is topic statement followed by elaboration and/or examples. The second frequently used structure is marked by clients beginning with an example, elaborating that example or giving others, and then stating a conclusion, interpretation, or diagnosis.

> Counselor: Share with me what it's like being you.
> Client: Wow! Just yesterday I was driving—carefully, I thought—past the school when. . . . Then my attorney called to tell me. . . . And to top that off, my malignancy is no longer in remission. Nothing seems to be going right!

There are some additional elements of structure that are important. These deal with whether content is focused primarily on the general versus the specific, others versus client, and the past versus the present.

Perhaps it is a simple element of content paraphrasing to pin down the focus whenever it is consistent; however, when clients jump from then to now to generalization to others to self to specific, it becomes necessary for counselors to separate, accumulate, sort, and paraphrase from each focus. For example: "Abortion is a bad thing, and people should be responsible enough to avoid relying on such a terrible thing just for personal convenience. Of course when a woman has been raped or the child will be deformed or unwanted, it is bad for the child, who would be better off not born. I knew a lady who never really recovered emotionally from her abortion. Really, I don't know how I can possibly cope with another child. The last one caused me six months of postpartum depression, and I don't want to go through that again. I really enjoyed the first one. Now all I feel is panic at the anticipation of this one being born."

Such client production is difficult to process but is made easier by separating the various focuses of time, degree of generality, others and self.

Traffic Signs

There are certain words, phrases, or sentences that are invitations to therapist emphasis and movement to a level deeper in the funnel. Generally, a repetition of these traffic signs or a vocal stress put on them in a paraphrase will elicit a deeper response from clients.

The following are some categories and examples of traffic signs:

Qualifiers

but	I guess	sometimes
sort of	maybe	might
a little	pretty much	not really

Generalizers

| it | they | people | that stuff |

Hiders

in others:	we	people do
	you	everybody
in time:	I was	someday
	I used to	I will
in blaming:	Because of him	I couldn't help it
	If it hadn't of been	If
	It wasn't my fault	I would be okay if

Traps

I have to	I should
I don't want to	I ought to
I don't know what to do	I must
either . . . or	I'll try

Emphases

| I insist | He'd better | or else |

Incongruences
   direct verbal contradictions
   incongruences between verbal and nonverbal responses
Vagueness
   weird   spacey
   neurotic   and everything

Here are some examples of a few client statements that include traffic signs.

"You know, when you walk into the tavern and pick up a pool cue, and you're the only woman at the table, everybody looks at you weird like they're thinking, 'What's she doing here? She doesn't belong.' And then you sort of choke and not shoot as well as you can."

"I really know what I'm doing, and I'm good at it, but sometimes my performance is really rotten. Mostly when they complain and all that stuff is when I do badly."

"She'd better come around soon or else!"

"I just have to go to San Francisco and see about that job, but working here isn't all that bad."

REFLECTION OF FEELING

Emotions, affect, feelings represent a part of people's experience. As such, they may be pleasant or unpleasant, simple or complex, polarized or marked by ambivalence. Generally speaking, well-adjusted people are aware of their feelings, and they express them in ways that are appropriate to the time and the circumstances.

Clients, not especially well-adjusted at least in the area for which they seek help, are often unaware of or confused by their emotions and hence do not manage them very well. Sometimes their only way of coping with an emotional nature is to suppress it and control the tendency toward expressing any feelings at all.

Emotional expression—the quality, degree of intensity, or unnatural absence—comprises one channel of communication. Quite naturally, people respond to obvious and strong emotional "statements" by approaching their source, if positive, or avoiding and defending against, if negative.

Reflection of feeling is basically the paraphrase of an emotional message. Being able to "mirror" client emotion (affect) by describing feelings in denotative terms (often referred to as labeling feelings) allows the client to be more aware of his/her feeling state and at the same time feel closer to the therapist who is so "understanding."

Sometimes a reflection of feeling is nothing more than a paraphrase of a connotative feeling statement. For example:

> *Client:* I'm really feeling bummed out by that last fight. She just doesn't fight fair. If she were at all logical, it would be easy to solve our problems.
>
> *Counselor:* You're very discouraged at your inability to communicate with her. Somehow her way of fighting confuses and irritates you.

Occasionally a reflection of feeling will be made from observation of a physical gesture or posture or facial motion. For example:

> Client clenches fist while talking about his/her father.
>
> *Counselor:* You're quite angry at him for doing that to you.
>
> *Or:* Even though that happened years ago, you're still mad at him.

> Client smiles while talking about advances by neighbor's husband.
>
> *Counselor:* It pleases you to be the object of a hustle.
>
> *Or:* Even though you think it's wrong to play around with another's husband, the thought of it is exciting to you.

Often there will be no words alluding to an emotional reaction or no physical manifestations of affect, and yet you, as therapist, suspect the presence of such emotions. Usually this impression comes from within you as you identify with the client's position. For example:

> Client is talking in a calm, semirelaxed voice about being held up last night at gunpoint.
>
> *Counselor:*   I bet you're still feeling some tension in your stomach—afraid, even though it is over.

Not always does a reflection of feeling have to be verbal. On occasion it may be helpful to mirror the posture or gesture of the client; even an exaggeration by the therapist of the client's action will draw the client's attention to the feeling state and to the therapist's awareness of it. Sometimes, by adopting the posture of the client, the therapist can facilitate awareness of the emotional state.

Formalizing Nonverbal Cues

One of the many channels of communication, itself rather complex, is that of nonverbal cues. This channel has received lots of popular notice (Fast, 1970; Hall, 1959) and is even afforded by some the status of an area of scientific inquiry called proxemics (Birdwhistell, 1952). Although the popular action may be mostly entertainment and the scientific status premature or overdone, there is value in therapy for the recognition of nonverbal cues.

Occasionally nonverbal behavior is the figure in the figure-ground framework; that is, it is intended to be the prominent mode of communication. Silence as a response to a direct and obvious question, gestures in the absence of verbal production, aggressive or inviting movements without words—these are all examples of nonverbal, focused communication.

Extreme care must be exercised in instances like these, for the message is derived more from the context than from the focus. There is far less universal acceptance of the meaning of nonverbal behavior than even connotative language; therefore, such nonverbal production should be paraphrased in very denotative language in order to establish proper understanding.

More often, nonverbal cues form part of the context of message transmission and serve principally to alter the intensity of the message (increase or decrease) and to validate or invalidate the spoken words. When this occurs, the preferred counselor action is to incorporate the qualitative aspect into a paraphrase of message or a reflection of feeling. For example:

> Client is clenching fists and gritting teeth while talking about unfair treatment by a parent.
> *Counselor:*   You're very angry at your mother.

In this sense nonverbal cues are not formalized but serve as very useful qualitative clues for the intended message. As such, they are extremely important and comprise one channel of communication that requires constant monitoring.

To formalize nonverbal cues, they must be brought to the attention of the client, moving them from ground to figure and processing their meaning. This is done when it seems that clients are separating their feeling selves from their intellectual selves or when the therapist wishes to confront clients with apparent inconsistencies. The following are some examples:

> *Counselor:*   You are saying that you're disturbed somewhat by his behavior, and you are gripping my hand so tightly that it feels like your fingernails are going clear through. You are more than somewhat disturbed.
> *Counselor:*   Your mouth is telling me that you are really worried, extremely concerned, very nearly panicked by what you must do, and yet your body appears relaxed, comfortable, without a tension anywhere. How do you explain such a contrast?

DESCRIPTION OF SITUATION

In the process of relating a circumstance, condition, or happening, it is quite natural for the teller to leave out considerable amounts of data. Those data vary from unimportant, through significant but common (hence easily overlooked), to highly important. The teller operates from a greater awareness of his/her situation and omits data because they seem insignificant, or obvious, or because the teller is focusing intently on something else.

One of the foremost propositions of perception is that the figure (focus) takes meaning or significance from the ground (background data) in which it is embedded.

The task of the therapist is to understand the circumstances, conditions, or happenings—in short, the situation—that is being incompletely described by the client. One way of validating that understanding is to infer and describe some of the parts missing in the narrative of the client. This is not as difficult as it may appear at first. It consists of the therapist putting him/herself in the circumstances of the client and "looking around." For example:

Client is a woman whose husband has just filed for divorce and there is reason for her to believe another woman is involved. Most of her comments are angry and hostile, directed at her husband.

Counselor says to self, "If I were in her situation, what would I be feeling? What would I be concerned about?"

Feelings and Concerns:
Anger toward husband
Love toward husband
Self-pity
What did I do wrong?
Where or how am I deficient to the extent he would want to replace me?
What has she got that I haven't?
How can I live without him?
I'll be better off without the rat.
I'll miss him a great deal.
What will happen to our children?
What'll I tell mama, the neighbors?
Will we have to sell the house and move?
If only he would come with me to counseling.
I should be strong and righteously indignant.

I feel weak and want him—or somebody—to make it feel better.

Another example:

Client is a college man who has been going with a girl back home for three years. He has just met and fallen "madly in love" with her cousin.

Counselor's thoughts in describing situation to him/herself: "He does have a problem. There are obviously three ways out. He can go back to the old girlfriend; he can go to the new one (her cousin!); or he can leave both of them. He could try to string them both along—dumb! How would I feel in this situation?

Feelings:
Ambivalent toward old girlfriend
  She has been good and faithful for three years.
  I do love her, I think—but if I loved her, why would I fall for her cousin?
  I don't want to hurt her.
  She does seem a little plain, and the old fire is not there any more.
Ambivalent toward self
  What kind of a creep am I? I can't just drop somebody who has stood by me for three years.
  On the other hand, it would be stupid to stay with her if I don't love her.
  Her cousin really rings my bell. I'd be foolish to let her get away.
  C'mon now, I've only known her for a week. How can I put so much weight on such a short time?
Ambivalent toward the cousin
  Wow! Is she a knockout! She could probably have any guy on campus.
  I wonder if she really cares for me, or if I'm just a pastime?
  Sure would be nice to spend forever with her.

> Maybe the fire will go out, and she'll be ordinary after a while.
>
> Why'd it have to be her cousin? Well, probably doesn't make any difference anyway.

Obviously the therapist should not assume that the client is experiencing exactly what is imagined; however, the therapist's vicarious experience can provide a framework for making gentle, tentative inferences. These are most effective in the form of paraphrases or incomplete leads; e.g., "Part of you would really like to hurt your husband for what he's doing, but another part . . ." or "How could I be so stupid, getting mixed up with her cousin? There must really be something loose in my head." Just as with an ordinary paraphrase or incomplete lead, the client will deny or correct it and move in a more accurate direction.

It is probably on the basis of descriptions of situations that a therapist can make careful, inferential leaps; that is, he/she can get out "in front of" the client, can move ahead of where the client is talking. If accurate, the inferential leap can save time and give the client an impression that the therapist *really* understands. If inaccurate or in error, the inferential leap will waste time and increase distance or create barriers between the therapist and client. A healthy degree of caution, small inferential leaps, and an air of tentativeness, therefore, are imperative in using this technique. An adage says that real artists paint in small strokes; likewise, real therapists infer in small leaps.

MANAGING THE TRACKING SKILLS

As was pointed our earlier, the essence of tracking is to hear messages by interpreting input from several channels of communication. It is important to realize that communication is a "two-way street" and that the therapist's actions have impact on the client. Table 3-1 gives the timing factors and rationale for the tracking skills.

The exact timing and intended purpose in using each skill will vary from client to client and from time to time with the same client. Much practice is required to develop mastery of

Table 3-1.   Managing Tracking Skills

Tracking skill	When to use	Rationale
Paraphrase of message	As soon as messages are apparent and frequently thereafter	Helps clients to clarify what is happening to them Increases client self-awareness Reinforces therapy process Strengthens therapeutic relationships
Structure of content	Early, as a refinement of summary of content	Clarifies topic statements from elaboration; conclusions from antecedent experiences Helps client toward messages, especially when responding to "traffic sign" clarification
Reflection of feeling	As feelings become apparent from client statements and behavior or when they seem to logically fit within the situation	Legitimizes feelings Helps clients to sharpen awareness of what they are experiencing emotionally Shows understanding by therapist
Formalizing nonverbal cues	When they directly transmit a major message When they validate verbalizations When they contradict verbalizations	Promotes client self-awareness Shows therapist's understanding Verification of messages and/or relative strength of message

Table 3-1. Managing Tracking Skills (Continued)

Tracking skill	When to use	Rationale
		Confrontation to clarify confusing messages and/or to cut through resistance
Description of situation	When enough clues are present to support cautious inferences and occasionally thereafter to sharpen understanding	Demonstrates therapist's understanding
		Shows clients that it is counterproductive to withhold information from therapists and from themselves

these skills properly, and even the experienced therapist must constantly monitor the effectiveness of each skill or combination of skills and be prepared to alter his/her approach the better to achieve the goals of therapy.

One of the frustrations for the neophyte counselor or student is knowing when to stress feelings, ideas, nonverbal messages, or situational cues. Being able to "hear" the various inputs is the first consideration. When several channels are carrying the same message, a counselor response to any one of them will probably be effective; but when a problem exists in the situation, when a high feeling state is present, and when the client is trying to understand what is happening, how does the counselor choose the channel that holds the most promise for movement toward resolution of the problem?

Experienced therapists seem to select the best or at least an acceptable response that provides smooth and rapid progress. They may do so because (a) they have developed a personal ability to conceptualize and communicate that is acceptable to most clients, or (b) they take a cue from the client for selection of the most productive response, or (c) they have a combination of conceptual ability and sensitivity.

There is room for variations in counselor style. It is probable that experienced therapists have developed an approach that is successful and comfortable for themselves. Possibly they have been conditioned by client response to those perceptions or cognitions that are most accurate or most helpful.

The approach may be based on logical abilities: the ability to receive, remember, and process concepts from what the client has said. Other therapists may rely more on aural input: the sensitivity to volume, stress, inflection, or pace of client verbalizations that gives cues to relative degrees of importance. Still other counselors may rely on visual signals—posture, rate or change of rate in breathing, color variations in complexion, eye movements—to help them select which lead to follow. Still others respond somewhat intuitively as a result of vicariously identifying with the client's circumstance and focus on whatever is prominent to their awareness.

One line of thought, neuro-linguistic programming (NLP) (Bandler & Grinder, 1975, 1979; Grinder and Bandler, 1976), suggests that clients provide clues not only for the focus of message but also for the kind of response they are primed to accept. It is postulated that clients develop a preference or style for dealing with their reality. The variations include the tendency for seeing, hearing, or feeling to dominate. Bandler and Grinder (1975) contend that experienced therapists of various theoretical persuasions respond as though they were tuning in on client verbal and eye-movement cues. Clients who use "see" verbs, as in "I see what you mean," and tend to look up in contemplation (up and right for constructing visual images, up and left for re-creating eidetic or remembered images) have a model that emphasizes seeing as a means to dealing with reality.

People who use "hear" verbs, as in "I hear what you're saying," and tend to look to the side or down and left in contemplation (to the right side for constructing auditory sounds or words, to the left side for remembering sounds or words, and down-left for processing auditory input) have a sound-centered model for functioning.

The use of "feel" verbs, as in "I feel okay about that," and the tendency to look down and to the right shows the preference for a kinesthetic (also smell and taste) bias for organizing experience and coping with reality.

If clients do indeed have a systematic bias, then communicating to them in a manner consistent with their bias will likely enhance the relationship and facilitate exploration. Because each bias has some inherent limitations, the direction for therapeutic correction may involve restructuring or reprogramming the client to operate occasionally within less-preferred styles.

The NLP system provides an organized means of selecting responses from the various channels of client communication. Because it is organized, it may be helpful for students to develop it as a base for further refinement.

SUMMARY OF MESSAGES

Only one word can be spoken at a time by clients, and similarly one piece of information is usually all that comes through the feeling channel and the nonverbal channel. Messages are structured one by one. Because of this linear nature of communication it is helpful to summarize periodically the areas of concern to the client.

An added reason for summaries is that client concerns are often multiple, they are confusing and difficult to define, and delineations between or among them are frequently blurred or nonexistent.

The occasional summary of messages allows both the client and the therapist to visualize the pattern formed by the separate messages and the interrelationships between messages. Obviously, the complexity of such patterns will vary greatly from client to client. A summary of messages for a relatively simple gestalt is as follows:

"You have described three major concerns that work against each other. First, you are not an extremely gifted student so that doing well requires great amounts of study. To make satisfactory progress and finish within five to six years you must put virtually all of your time into school work.

"Second, you are not wealthy, you have borrowed more money than you're comfortable about, and so you must work to maintain yourself and to pay for college expenses. Any time spent working is time away from your studies.

"And third, you are a human being with needs for social interaction, variety, recreation, and occasional rest. Putting all of your energy and time into school and work leaves none for emotional regeneration, and so you feel depressed emotionally and physically drained most of the time. This in turn decreases your effectiveness both in school and at work."

Even though "relatively simple," the concerns of this client are multiple and difficult. Obviously, continued exploration and processing are necessary.

An example of a more complex summary of message is as follows:

"Let me see if I'm understanding your position. You are married to one person, but you have been living separately for several years. He does not want a divorce but is doing nothing to get you back together. So one problem is to resolve your present marriage, but there are several subproblems: (a) your needs are not being met in your marriage; (b) you've given him the power position by refusing to take any initiative; obviously he is more satisfied with the status quo than you are, or he would do something to change it; (c) you're afraid to take action because you might drive him away; you're not happy the way things are, but they could be worse.

"A second major problem is that you have a friend to whom you are strongly attracted, but you're not sure of that relationship because you fear it's based on your strong need for someone. If you didn't need so much, he might not be so attractive.

"Third, while you didn't intend to become physically involved and so took no precautions, you fear you are pregnant. This aggravates the other problems because (a) your present husband told you to 'not get pregnant' and being so will reduce your chances of working things out with him; (b) you're not sure of your relationship with the other man, so marrying him for the baby's sake would be foolish; but if the relationship really is potentially good, not marrying him would be foolish. Mostly, you don't want to be trapped into or out of any marriage.

"A fourth complication is the fact that you work at the same place as this other man, and if the boss were to know what was happening, he would probably terminate your job. Since you are a probationary employee, you would have no recourse but to accept his action.

"Fifth, you have really come down hard on yourself for (a) being unfaithful to your husband; (b) foolishly getting pregnant and going through the torment of deciding how to manage this circumstance; (c) rehashing how you have been a disappointment to your parents, yourself—everybody; (d) bringing up the feelings of how much better your sister has run her life; (e) reliving the unresolved feelings of your earlier illegitimate births and subsequent adoptions of your children."

Although such summaries often contain overwhelming problems, they do clarify circumstances and provide the groundwork for a series of therapeutic interventions. It might be good to point out at this time that such complex circumstances do not lend themselves to a single therapeutic intervention strategy. When the circumstances are completely identified, it is possible that techniques involving behavior modification, value restructuring, affective integration, and social training may all apply to the same client. In such cases a therapist must be cautious so as to avoid using simultaneously two methods which will counter each other.

Table 3-2.   Managing Tracking Skills (Continued)

Tracking skill	When to use	Rationale
Summary of messages	Occasionally as part of processing	Formalizes the real problem
	When things bog down	Separates components of complex situations into soluble pieces
	When making transition into solution analysis	
	At end of session	Leveling and "calling the shots" as you see them
	If contradictory, as a means of confronting the client with double messages	Bottom lining
		Helps make transitions from session to session or between parts of the process

Table 3-2, an extension of Table 3-1, gives timing and rationale for the summary of messages.

SUMMARY

Perhaps the most dynamic and most helpful part of the entire therapy process is tracking. Without the help of a skilled therapist, clients tend to wander around in the relatively superficial content and incorrect conclusion area at the "lip of the funnel." The tracking skills of paraphrase of message, structure of content, reflection of feelings, formalization of nonverbal cues, description of situation, and summary of messages are systematically employed to verify meanings and to encourage deeper exploration on the part of the client.

Paraphrase of message is used as soon as messages are apparent and frequently thereafter. Its purposes are to help the clients clarify what is happening to them, increase client self-awareness, reinforce the therapy process, and strengthen the therapeutic relationship.

Structure of content is a transitional skill between processing of content and processing of messages. It is used early as a refinement of summary of content. Its effect is to clarify relationships among client statements and to move toward focus on messages.

Reflection of feeling is used when feelings become obvious from client statements and behavior, or when they seem to fit logically within the situation. This skill demonstrates that feelings are a legitimate part of life and of therapy, helps clients to sharpen awareness of what they are experiencing emotionally, and demonstrates understanding on the part of the therapist.

Formalization of nonverbal cues consists of drawing the client's attention to such behavior and denotatively describing the therapist's interpretation or confusion as to its meaning. This skill is employed under three conditions:

1. When the cues directly transmit a major message. This promotes client self-awareness and shows understanding on the part of the therapist.

2. When the cues validate verbalizations; i.e., when they are congruent with the spoken messages. The message is verified by this technique, and gradations of intensity can be reflected.
3. When the cues contradict verbalizations; i.e., when they are inconsistent or incongruent with the spoken messages. Formalizing the cues in this instance provides a confrontation with the client and generally serves to clarify confusing messages or to cut through client resistance.

When enough clues are presented to support cautious inferences, the therapist may go beyond the client's disclosures and verbalize inferences about what must be going on. This is called description of situation. When done properly, it is very powerful in demonstrating the therapist's understanding of the client's predicament and in showing the client that it is counterproductive to withhold information from either the therapist or him/herself.

Summary of messages is employed occasionally as part of processing, when things bog down, when making transition into analysis of potential solutions, and at the end of a session. This serves to formalize real problems from less significant data; separates the component parts of complex situations, thus permitting resolution of subparts and analysis of the relationships between subparts; provides "bottom line" statements of what the therapist sees; and aids in making transitions between and within sessions.

By virtue of their seeking help, clients are not able to clarify, analyze, and resolve circumstances with which they are faced. Left to their own devices, they probably will repeat past errors. Tracking is the process by which a therapist monitors multiple channels of communication and teaches clients to observe and understand the meaning of their own experience.

Exercises

This portion of the book will provide two sections of exercises dealing with tracking skills. The first is quite easy, the second more difficult. Each section will be followed by answers and examples for that section.

Simple Exercises
Comparison responses begin on page 91.

I. Paraphrase of message
   A. Write a paraphrase of message for each of the client statements in the exercises for chapter 2, page 50.
   B. Write a paraphrase of message for the following:
      1. Sometimes I think that he's wrong and unfair in his demands, but mostly he's pretty much right on.
      2. Saturdays are such a drag! There is never anything worthwhile to do, so I watch lots of TV.
      3. Don't you think that there are lots of criminals in government positions?
      4. I just don't know what we'll do if our welfare allotment is cut back any more like it was last month.
      5. In my daydreams I'm always incredibly successful. Every proposal I make gets accepted and turns into a real moneymaker. That could really happen if I'd ever get even one proposal finished and submitted.
      6. Taxes are a real pain! I never know for sure what to deduct, so I guess at it and then live in fear for months that the IRS will audit me and find something wrong.
   C. For the same client statements as in I-B select, from the counselor responses that follow, the best paraphrase of message.
      1. Sometimes I think that he's wrong and unfair in his demands, but mostly he's pretty much right on.
         (a) He is really insensitive and selfish.
         (b) Living with another person can be extremely trying.

    (c)   Most of the time you agree with him; occasionally there is disagreement.

    (d)   Only unreasonable variations warrant complaints.

2. Saturdays are such a drag! There is never anything worthwhile to do, so I watch lots of TV.

    (a)   It would be better to have school on Saturdays.

    (b)   Kid's cartoons really aren't very inspiring.

    (c)   Saturday housecleaning turns you off.

    (d)   When there is nothing important or exciting to do, you fill time with TV.

3. Don't you think that there are lots of criminals in government positions?

    (a)   You're wondering if I think that politicians are crooked.

    (b)   You are concerned with corruption in government.

    (c)   If we paid them more, they wouldn't have to steal.

    (d)   No. I think politicians are very honest.

4. I just don't know what we'll do if our welfare allotment is cut back any more like it was last month.

    (a)   You are just barely managing on the money you get now.

    (b)   It's not fair to punish welfare people just because the economy is in a slump.

    (c)   It's no fun being on welfare.

    (d)   You don't have a large enough lot now, and with less you'd have to find somewhere else to plant your carrots.

5. In my daydreams I'm always incredibly successful. Every proposal I make gets accepted and turns into a real moneymaker. That could happen in reality if I'd ever get even one proposal finished and submitted.

    (a)   For people who don't succeed, it's nice that they can daydream.

(b)   You are preventing your own success by not finishing and testing your proposals.

(c)   Sure would be nice if you weren't so lazy.

(d)   In reality one has to be a good salesperson to get ahead.

6.   Taxes are a real pain! I never know for sure what to deduct, so I guess at it and then live in fear for months that the IRS will audit me and find something wrong.

(a)   Your lack of knowledge and guessing strategy cause you considerable emotional turmoil.

(b)   A flat-rate income tax would solve all your problems.

(c)   If tax forms weren't confusing, there would be lots of accountants and attorneys out of work.

(d)   I just use the standard deduction.

II.   Structure of content

A.   For the following excerpts identify the topic and the elaboration; write a paraphrase that accounts for the structure.

1.   My friend says I'm too compulsive, but I think she's just touchy. Of course I like to have a clean apartment and do go a little crazy when she drops cigarette ashes on the carpet. And those glass rings on the piano. You'd think she could use a coaster; goodness knows I have plenty of them tucked around the place. I was taught to get up promptly at six a.m. and make the bed and get on with breakfast. The other night when she stayed at my place—do you know? She stayed in bed until seven thirty and then didn't even offer to make the bed or help with breakfast.

2.   I really failed that test—didn't finish the last question and totally misunderstood three others. Probably that was because I've not been eating regularly since getting fired from my job. I re-

ally didn't falsify the records like they claim I did; it was just that I came up short about $40 and didn't know how to account for it. My mind was somewhat nonfunctional, probably because of Dad's accident and three weeks unconscious and in intensive care. I just can't seem to generate enough energy to really care; I'm so depressed.

3. People are really pathetic nowadays. There was only a 43 percent turnout for the last election, and it was an important one. And the meeting for input to the city planning commission was called off after ten minutes because no one came. United Fund donations are down again; even the spring marathon is getting third-page news coverage because not many people have registered.

B. For the same client statements as in II-A, select from the counselor responses that follow, the best structural paraphrase.

1. My friend says I'm too compulsive, but I think she's just touchy. Of course I like to have a clean apartment and do go a little crazy when she drops cigarette ashes on the carpet. And those glass rings on the piano. You'd think she could use a coaster; goodness knows I have plenty of them tucked around the place. I was taught to get up promptly at six a.m. and make the bed and get on with breakfast. The other night when she stayed at my place—do you know? She stayed in bed until seven thirty and then didn't even offer to make the bed or help with breakfast.

(a) You're wondering whether or not you're compulsive. The differences between your living style and your friend's—namely, tidiness with ashes and glass rings, morning schedule and routine—are things that suggest either your compulsiveness or her intolerance.

(b) People who drop ashes and sleep until seven thirty have no room to criticize. She is just a slob.

(c) It's important to take good care of things, what with the high costs today; therefore, it's perfectly normal to express a high degree of emotion when someone drops ashes on the floor or doesn't use a coaster or make the bed promptly.

(d) You don't believe you're compulsive, because you plan everything well in advance and do everything according to plan—like getting up at the same time every day and keeping a tidy apartment. You never do any "spur of the moment" or wildly spontaneous things, so it's hard to see how your friend can call you compulsive.

2. I really failed that test—didn't finish the last question and totally misunderstood three others. Probably that was because I've not been eating regularly since getting fired from my job. I really didn't falsify the records like they claim I did; it was just that I came up short about $40 and didn't know how to account for it. My mind was somewhat nonfunctional, probably because of Dad's accident and three weeks unconscious and in intensive care. I just can't seem to generate enough energy to really care; I'm so depressed.

(a) The real problem is your father's accident, which caused you to make a mistake at work, get into trouble and lose your job, eat poorly, and fail the test.

(b) Not having any energy results from not eating. When you're physically down, nothing goes right.

    (c)   You are depressed and find it difficult to care as a result of so many things going wrong—your father's accident, the job difficulty and getting fired, and the failed test.

    (d)   Don't worry. You'll work it out. Other people have fathers who die, go to jail for false records, flunk out of school, and suffer from malnutrition, and they live through it.

3. People are really pathetic nowadays. There was only a 43 percent turnout for the last election, and it was an important one. And the meeting for input to the city planning commission was called off after ten minutes because no one came. United Fund donations are down again; even the spring marathon is getting third-page news coverage because not many people have registered.

    (a)   There is no hope for a society that will not even support a spring marathon.

    (b)   You've concluded that apathy is a problem now because of the poor responses to the election, the planning meeting, United Fund donations, and the spring marathon.

    (c)   Low voter turnout, a canceled meeting, a decrease in donations, and third-page coverage of a sporting event causes you to say that society is sick.

    (d)   Isn't it pathetic how irresponsible people are? Truck drivers go on strike; teachers want more money; and doctors are getting sued for malpractice.

C. From the following client statements list the traffic signs and tell what kind they are:

1. Sometimes I get really discouraged.
2. I suppose it will work out.
3. He is really weird.
4. I always behave responsibly except when I'm sick.
5. That stuff can really cause problems.

6. I just have to confront her about it.
7. I used to really care for him.
8. They're not so bad, I guess.
9. If it hadn't have been for that umpire, I would have won the game.
10. Well, he'd better come through with the money!

III. Reflection of feeling
   A. Write a reflection of feeling for each of the client statements in the exercises for chapter 2, section II page 50.
   B. Write a reflection of feeling for the following:
      1. I haven't seen him for four months, and I can hardly wait another minute for him to get home.
      2. Why should I try anymore? Nothing is going to change.
      3. That #@!!*# creep! I'd really like to alter his face!
      4. She did a fantastic job. I've never seen anyone operate more smoothly.
      5. Would I ever like a figure like hers! She attracts men like an overripe peach draws fruit flies.
      6. I think maybe I could do it if you'd help me a little more.
   C. Compare your reflections of feeling with the following examples and select the best for each example.
      1. I haven't seen him for four months, and I can hardly wait another minute for him to get home.
         (a) You think it will be nice to have him home.
         (b) There is a certain quality of anticipation as you contemplate his return.
         (c) You are really excited about his coming.
         (d) Obviously you love him a great deal.
      2. Why should I try anymore? Nothing is going to change.
         (a) It's more than a little discouraging to you.
         (b) You think there is no value in another attempt.
         (c) You would like to succeed but doubt that you can.

       (d)   It's easier to feel sorry for yourself than to work at it.

   3.   That #@!!*# creep! I'd really like to alter his face!

       (a)   He is a good candidate for plastic surgery.

       (b)   You are awfully angry at him.

       (c)   People who are that creepy should change their face.

       (d)   He'd be a real hit at a Halloween party.

   4.   She did a fantastic job. I've never seen anyone operate more smoothly.

       (a)   She really did a nice job.

       (b)   You're impressed by her performance.

       (c)   You feel that she is really an expert.

       (d)   It would be nice if others did as well.

   5.   Would I ever like a figure like hers! She attracts men like an overripe peach draws fruit flies.

       (a)   It's not fair for her to get all those men.

       (b)   You feel angry at her for her attractive figure.

       (c)   You are afraid she will steal your fiancé.

       (d)   You are envious, or maybe a little jealous of her.

   6.   I think maybe I could do it if you'd help me a little more.

       (a)   You're hesitant to try it on your own.

       (b)   You won't do it unless I help.

       (c)   It's my job to make you successful.

       (d)   You're ashamed of your past performance.

IV. Description of situation

Put yourself in the situations that are incompletely described below. Write three ideas or feelings that would be important to you in each of those circumstances. Check your responses against those in the section on comparison responses.

   A.   The governor of your state has just called and asked you to serve on an important advisory committee.

   B.   The doctor informed you that the tests confirmed that you have cancer.

    C.   You have confirmed that your lottery ticket is the million-dollar winner.

Comparison Responses

  I. Paraphrase of message
      A.   Compare your paraphrases of message for the client statements in the chapter 2 exercises with these:
          1.   You have managed poorly in regard to financial matters and are now forced to admit your failure to your father and to yourself.
          2.   Basically you're faced with a relationship you want and can't have and with one you have and don't want.
          3.   Even though you want to remain neutral, you find yourself drawn into the conflict of your parents' divorce.
          4.   For some reason it's necessary for you to defend being thirty-three and unmarried.
          5.   Because you have been unable to cope with teasing, you are considering changing your goal.
          6.   Your sister's behavior is a problem for you but not for her.
      B.   You can compare your responses to those in I-C of the exercises as well as considering the following analyses of the statements. Paraphrases of message may be made in varying ways, so allow for some effectiveness in your own even though they are not identical with the key.
          1.   Two parts to the statement; incongruent meanings; three traffic signs; *sometimes, mostly, pretty much;* paraphrase of message reflects implied emphasis.
          2.   A blaming attitude that indicates external frame of reference; major statement: "I watch lots of [too much] TV."
          3.   Questions often conceal statements, especially those that begin with "Don't you think?"

4. The message of the present is hidden in reference to the future.
5. The traffic signal, *if,* allows the message to be hidden in blaming—"I would be okay if . . ."
6. The focus is on taxes, and blame is placed on the system: It's their fault I'm suffering. The major message is that a performance on my part leads to an undesirable outcome.

C. 1. (c); 2. (d); 3. (b); 4. (a); 5. (b); 6. (a).

II. Structure of content

A. The topic sentence or thesis statement is given first, then the elaboration of it.

1. Topic: My friend says I'm compulsive.
    Elaboration (in this case, challenges to topic sentence):
    I like a clean apartment.
    I go crazy when she drops ashes.
    I get upset at glass rings on the piano.
    I have coasters in necessary places.
    I get up promptly and early; she sleeps in.

2. Topic: I'm so depressed (topic in conclusion form).
    Elaboration (I'm depressed because——):
    I failed that test.
    I've not been eating regularly.
    I got fired.
    I came up short by $40.
    My dad had an accident and is unconscious.

3. Topic: People are really pathetic nowadays.
    Elaboration:
    A 43 percent election turnout.
    A canceled planning commission meeting.
    United Fund donations are down.
    Poor registration for spring marathon.

B. 1. (a); 2. (c); 3. (b).

   Note: There may be some confusion on item 3 because of the word *pathetic.* In the context of the client statement as judged from elaborations, the client probably misused the word and would have said "apathetic" if denotatively correct. Since each of the elaboration elements described apathy, response (b) is the correct one.

C. Traffic signs
   1. sometimes (qualifier)
   2. suppose, it (qualifier, generalizer)
   3. weird (vagueness)
   4. direct verbal contradiction
   5. that stuff (generalizer)
   6. have to, it (trap, generalizer)
   7. used to (hider in time)
   8. they, I guess (generalizer, qualifier)
   9. If it hadn't have been (hider in blaming)
   10. he'd better (emphasis)

III. Reflection of feeling
   A. Compare your reflections of feeling for the client statements in the chapter 2 exercises with these:
      1. You're embarrassed to admit that you've managed poorly.
      2. It's very frustrating to have what you don't want and to want what you can't have.
      3. You're angry at your parents for fighting through you.
      4. You're a little anxious yourself about not being married. *Or:* You resent it when others are critical of your being single.
      5. You're quite discouraged.
      6. You're worried about your sister.
   B. Compare your reflections of feeling to the keyed response for III-C. Remember that slight variations may still be effective and that even an incorrect response often elicits a correction from the client.
   C. 1. (c); 2. (a); 3. (b); 4. (b); 5. (d); 6. (a).

IV. Description of situation
   Compare your lists of three ideas or feelings to see if they are similar to those contained in the following lists:
   A. Governor's advisory committee
      Why me? Where'd he get my name?
      Wow! I must be important!

I wonder how much work will be involved.

Will travel and other expenses be paid?

I should not worry about reimbursement. This is an opportunity to give and to serve.

The family will be proud of me.

I wonder if I'm really capable enough.

I don't really want to do it. I'm too scared.

B.   Cancer

Why me?

I don't want to die.

Maybe it's not that serious.

There must be a mistake. I need a second opinion.

Who will look after the children?

I'll go to Mexico and get cured.

I'm too young to die.

How long do I have left?

Will the insurance pay for treatment?

I'll lick it. It won't get the best of me.

C.   Million-dollar winner

Hooray!

I don't believe it. I hope it's true.

I'm rich! I can quit that lousy job.

What am I going to do with a million dollars?

Better not spend any till I get it for sure.

The government will take most of it anyway.

I really don't need it. It will just complicate my life.

Wow! I can get out of debt.

I think I'll buy a sports car.

Exercises of a More Difficult Nature
Comparison responses begin on page 105.

I.   Paraphrase of message

A.   Write a paraphrase of message for the following:

1.   When people ask me where I went to high school, I get tensed up. Harris High School is where all the delinquents and slow kids are sent.

2.   It's so hard for me to get close to people. I want

to be liked so much, and yet my conversations with people seem so superficial and empty.

3. I thought he liked me, that we had something special going, but when I asked him to meet my parents, he made an excuse about why he couldn't do that. He's been very cold toward me since.

4. I just don't understand it. My grades are okay in everything except my major. Usually I work hard to get all the less important homework done, then I have two or three hours, between ten p.m. and one a.m. to do my chemistry and trig. I work so hard on them, over and over again, but I just can't seem to get them.

5. I'm through for the season; maybe for good. The doctor said the operation went okay but that rehabilitation will be hard and will take a long time. Oh well, football isn't everything. I can be an outstanding accountant or a rich banker.

6. Sure, I drink the hard stuff occasionally. Just last week I tied one on like you'd never believe, but I can handle it. All that stuff about out-of-control drinking, booze in the morning, drinking alone—I've done all of those, and I'm just fine, just fine.

B. For the same client statements as in I-A, select, from the counselor responses that follow, the best paraphrase of message.

1. When people ask me where I went to high school, I get tensed up. Harris High School is where all the delinquents and slow kids are sent.
   (a) It's nobody's business where you went to high school.
   (b) You're not very proud of your actions during school.
   (c) High school has some bad memories for you.

     (d)   Graduating from a good school helps your image.

2.   It's so hard for me to get close to people. I want to be liked so much, and yet my conversations with people seem so superficial and empty.

    (a)   People don't find you to be very likable.

    (b)   If only you were an interesting conversationalist, then people would like you.

    (c)   You are emotionally isolated and don't know what to do about it.

    (d)   It's hard to get close to people like you want to. People are just not interested in talking about important matters.

3.   I thought he liked me, that we had something special going, but when I asked him to meet my parents, he made an excuse about why he couldn't do that. He's been very cold toward me since.

    (a)   I assumed too much, and now I have alienated him.

    (b)   I just know he'd like my folks. Why is he being difficult?

    (c)   It wasn't that I expected to get married right away. Those things take time.

    (d)   I wonder if he is interested in someone else.

4.   I just don't understand it. My grades are okay in everything except my major. Usually I work hard to get all the less important homework done, then I have two or three hours, between ten p.m. and one a.m. to do my chemistry and trig. I work so hard on them, over and over again, but I just can't seem to get them.

    (a)   You're not very smart in chemistry and trigonometry.

    (b)   You have a mental block when it comes to homework in your major.

    (c)   Studying so late is interfering with your social life, and you resent having to do it.

    (d)   The studying you do while you're fresh is

producing better results than that which
you put off till last.

5. I'm through for the season; maybe for good.
The doctor said the operation went okay but
that rehabilitation will be hard and will take a
long time. Oh well, football isn't everything. I
can be an outstanding accountant or a rich
banker.

(a) Your attitude is healthy because you know
that football isn't everything.

(b) It's hard to talk yourself out of the disappointment you're feeling.

(c) What's really important is succeeding at
whatever you do.

(d) Years from now being a football player
won't seem so important.

6. Sure, I drink the hard stuff occasionally. Just last
week I tied one on like you'd never believe, but I
can handle it. All that stuff about out-of-control drinking, booze in the morning, drinking
alone—I've done all of those, and I'm just fine,
just fine.

(a) You don't believe all that stuff about drinking being bad for you.

(b) Even though drinking is bad for others,
you can handle it okay.

(c) There are alcoholics, and there are drunks.
You're just a drunk.

(d) Your drinking is causing you some concern. Maybe you aren't handling it as well
as you'd like to believe.

II. Structure of content

A. For the following excerpts identify the topic and elaboration; write a paraphrase that accounts for the
structure.

1. Do you think that television is really a healthy influence on children? Why, the other day I saw a
program that showed children taking candy
from a variety store, and when their parents

were confronted with the evidence, all they said was "It's no big deal. All kids steal things." Shoplifting is one of the most costly crimes to our society, and employee theft is big too. I watched a series that showed how even top executives take company goods and squander resources selfishly. Television is showcasing criminal behavior.

2. This morning I had a major dilemma in deciding which shirt to wear with which slacks. Then my roommate said, "Do you want Wheaties or Corn Chex for breakfast?" I said, "You choose." My biology prof said we could do a term paper or an experiment for extra credit, and I'm not doing well in the class, so I really ought to do one or the other, but I'm not sure I want to do either of them. The holidays are almost here. I could go home, but it's so quiet on campus, and I could save money and get a start on next quarter's reading, but I'd sort of like to see the old gang, except that I don't know who is going to be there this year. Somehow life wouldn't be such a hassle if I didn't have so many decisions to make.

3. I'll tell you what it is. I'm just not cut out to be an architect. They have to do all of those calculations and messing around with formulas. Of course, I've always had a knack for numbers, and I guess any job includes some uninteresting aspects. Sitting at a drawing board for long periods really gets to me, too. But of course, architects have luxurious offices and nice surroundings and usually deal with impressive people. I have some great ideas in designing living space, so you see, with my facility with numbers and talent for artistic expression, I'll probably be a great architect someday.

B. For the same client statements as in II-A select from the counselor responses that follow the best structural paraphrase.

1. Do you think that television is really a healthy influence on children? Why, the other day I saw a program that showed children taking candy from a variety store, and when their parents were confronted with the evidence, all they said was "It's no big deal. All kids steal things." Shoplifting is one of the most costly crimes to our society, and employee theft is big too. I watched a series that showed how even top executives take company goods and squander resources selfishly. Television is showcasing criminal behavior.

   (a) Television is showing off criminal behavior. For example, there were the programs on shoplifting plus an attitude of "It's nothing to be concerned about."

   (b) You believe that television has a bad influence on children because it focuses on criminal behavior, like employee theft and children's shoplifting plus an attitude of "It's nothing to be concerned about."

   (c) Stealing is no big deal, and showing it on television is okay because that's what people like to watch.

   (d) There is a high degree of criminality in our society, and television does a pretty accurate job of portraying it, so I think that television has a beneficial impact on children.

2. This morning I had a major dilemma in deciding which shirt to wear with which slacks. Then my roommate said, "Do you want Wheaties or Corn Chex for breakfast?" I said, "You choose." My biology prof said we could do a term paper or an experiment for extra credit, and I'm not doing well in the class, so I really ought to do one or the other, but I'm not sure I want to do either of them. The holidays are almost here. I could go home, but it's so quiet on campus, and I could save money and get a start on next quarter's reading, but I'd sort of like to see the old gang,

except that I don't know who is going to be there this year. Somehow life wouldn't be such a hassle if I didn't have so many decisions to make.

(a) Life is made up of many decisions, some of which are important, others less significant. Some important ones for you relate to extra credit in biology and going home for the holidays. Of less importance are which clothing to wear and which cereal to eat for breakfast.

(b) Roommates and biology professors should be more decisive in running their affairs. I have enough decisions to make without taking on the results of their ineffectuality.

(c) The really big issue for you is having the old group of friends disintegrate as each goes his own separate way. Going home is just not as much fun as it used to be.

(d) You have great difficulty in making decisions. Not only is it hard to determine the best choice of extra-credit project or even whether or not to do one, but simpler decisions like going home for the holidays, what clothes to wear, and even which of two cereals to eat are big obstacles in your life.

3. I'll tell you what it is. I'm just not cut out to be an architect. They have to do all of those calculations and messing around with formulas. Of course, I've always had a knack for numbers, and I guess any job includes some uninteresting aspects. Sitting at a drawing board for long periods really gets to me, too. But of course, architects have luxurious offices and nice surroundings and usually deal with impressive people. I have some great ideas in designing living space, so you see, with my facility with numbers and talent for artistic expression, I'll probably be a great architect someday.

     (a)   Architecture is a bad career for you because you don't like math and you dislike sitting at the drawing board.

     (b)   Architecture is a good career for you because, even though you don't like math and dislike sitting at the drawing table, math is easy, and you are talented artistically.

     (c)   A part of you rebels at the drudgery of computing and slaving away at the drawing table, while another part takes pride in artistic skills and facility with math, so you are confused relative to your proposed career.

     (d)   Once you are successful enough to have an assistant who computes and draws, you will truly be a happy architect.

C.   From the following client statements list the traffic signs and tell what kind they are:

    1.   Probably you will think I'm weird, but I sort of get excited over that stuff.

    2.   People say that I should broaden my interests, and I suppose that someday I will.

    3.   They say that someday I will regret not having moved on it sooner, but I don't know what to do.

    4.   If I could just get started, maybe I would be successful so someday I might pull it off.

    5.   That pretty much sums it up. I used to be okay, so I suppose I will catch on to that stuff if I try.

III. Reflection of feelings

    A.   Write a reflection of feeling for each of the client statements in the paraphrase exercise on page 94.

    B.   Write a reflection of feeling for the following:

       1.   I'm four weeks pregnant. My boyfriend won't marry me, and abortion is out; I don't really want a baby, at least not until I'm out of high school, but I can't stand the thought of giving it to some stranger. What am I going to do?!

       2.   The disease is progressive. Unless the doctors can achieve remission of symptoms, I will be totally dependent on my wife within two years. I

would rather be dead than to be a burden on her.

3. He's been dead for three years now, but I can still remember how he looked that last Christmas; he was so happy, and he made me feel like a schoolgirl again.

4. Sometimes I have strange thoughts, things I could never tell anybody else. Does that mean I'm crazy?

5. All I do is watch TV. I walk in the room and automatically flick on the set. Four or five hours later my work is not done; I've wasted all that time. What is the matter with me?

6. And then, I don't know what came over me, but I hit her! Again and again I hit her! Initially she cried, like any three-year-old would do, but then she just sort of lay there, whimpering to herself. What kind of a person would beat a child? What kind of a creep am I?

C. Compare your reflections of feeling with the following examples, and select the best for each example.

1. I'm four weeks pregnant. My boyfriend won't marry me, and abortion is out; I don't really want a baby, at least not until I'm out of high school, but I can't stand the thought of giving it to some stranger. What am I going to do?!

    (a) You're angry at your boyfriend for deserting you.

    (b) You feel trapped and sort of panicky.

    (c) You're upset because this happened while you are still in high school.

    (d) You feel frightened at having to do it all on your own.

2. The disease is progressive. Unless the doctors can achieve remission of symptoms, I will be totally dependent on my wife within two years. I would rather be dead than to be a burden on her.

    (a) It's hard not to feel sorry for yourself.

    (b)   You're angry at the doctors for not curing you.

    (c)   You're mad at God for letting this happen to you.

    (d)   You feel sorry for your wife.

3. He's been dead for three years now, but I can still remember how he looked that last Christmas; he was so happy, and he made me feel like a schoolgirl again.

    (a)   The thought of your husband makes you sad again.

    (b)   You're grateful that he was such a good person.

    (c)   It's just no fun at all to be a widow.

    (d)   You miss him but still get happiness from his memory.

4. Sometimes I have strange thoughts, things I could never tell anybody else. Does that mean I'm crazy?

    (a)   It's exciting to have weird thoughts.

    (b)   You're frustrated at not being able to share your thoughts.

    (c)   It's scary to have such thoughts; you're not sure of your sanity.

    (d)   You're a little curious as to whether or not you are crazy.

5. All I do is watch TV. I walk in the room and automatically flick on the set. Four or five hours later my work is not done; I've wasted all that time. What is the matter with me?

    (a)   You're pretty well disgusted with yourself over this TV habit.

    (b)   You're afraid that you have TV addicition.

    (c)   Wasting time makes you feel guilty.

    (d)   You're ashamed to admit that the tube has control over you.

6. And then, I don't know what came over me, but I hit her! Again and again I hit her! Initially she cried, like any three-year-old would do, but then

she just sort of lay there, whimpering to herself. What kind of a person would beat a child? What kind of a creep am I?

- (a) Whatever she did made you extremely angry.
- (b) You're puzzled about the personal characteristics of a child beater.
- (c) Because child abusers were abused by their parents, you're upset with your mother for making you do this.
- (d) You're very sorry for what happened and very much ashamed of yourself for doing it.

IV. Description of situation

Put yourself in the situations that are incompletely described below. Write as many ideas or feelings as you can that would be important to you in each of those circumstances. Then check your lists against those in the response section.

- A. You have been in a serious automobile accident that affected your spinal cord in the lumbar region, leaving you paralyzed from the waist down.
- B. After 15 years of fidelity to your spouse, you find yourself caught in an affair with your next-door neighbor.
- C. You are the oldest child in a family with three younger sisters. For two years your father has been engaging you in incestuous activities.
- D. At Grange High School you were a student-body officer and a starter on the basketball team. After transferring to Urban Mammoth High School you refuse even to try out for any sports or activities.
- E. You've been separated from your wife and family for 12 months because of a remote work assignment. Next week you will return home.
- F. Your husband has a violent temper, especially when he has been drinking. He beats you frequently and sometimes severely. You are at the battered-women's shelter following one of the more severe beatings.

    G.   You're engaged to a person who is of a different race and religion from yours. Your parents are adamantly opposed to your marrying him.

    H.   You are a third-quarter junior, and you are flunking out of school.

    I.   Your spouse and two of your three children have just been killed in a fire that destroyed your home.

V. The other tracking skills, along with most of the general enhancing skills in the following chapter, do not lend themselves to paper-and-pencil exercises. Careful review of the text and coached experiences in the presence of an accomplished therapist or trainer is the best procedure for mastering them.

Comparison Responses

I. Paraphrase of message
   - A. Compare your paraphrases of message with those keyed correct in I-B as well as considering the following analyses of the statements:
     1. Implication: If I attended Harris High, it was probably because I was either delinquent or slow or both.
     2. Emphasis: I am not close to people.
     3. The key is *thought,* with an implication of *thought wrongly.*
     4. Emphasis: Okay in everything *except.*
     5. Focus: I'm through; football *isn't* everything. When focus is on the negative *(isn't),* the message is often opposite to what's stated.
     6. Emphasis: I can handle it. If it weren't a problem, it wouldn't need handling, and I wouldn't need to convince myself.
   - B. 1. (b); 2. (c); 3. (a); 4. (d); 5. (b); 6. (d).

II. Structure of content
   - A. The topic sentence or thesis statement is given first, then the elaboration of it.
     1. Topic: Television is an unhealthy influence on children.

Elaboration: Children taking candy; parents condoning children's stealing; employee theft.

2. Topic: Life wouldn't be such a hassle if I didn't have so many decisions to make. (The message is that I have trouble making decisions.)

Elaboration: What clothes to wear; what cereal to eat; whether or not to do an assignment; whether or not to go home for holidays.

3. Topics (there are two): I'm not cut out to be an architect; I'll probably be a great architect.

Elaboration: I don't like computing; I don't like drawing; I am good at computing; I am artistic.

B. 1. (b); 2. (d); 3. (c).

C. Traffic signs

1. probably (qualifier), weird (vagueness), but (qualifier), sort of (qualifier), that stuff (generalizer)

2. people (generalizer), I should (trap), suppose (qualifier), someday I will (hider in time)

3. they (generalizer), someday (hider in time), I will (hider in time), it (generalizer), but (qualifier), I don't know what to do (trap)

4. if (hider in blaming), maybe (qualifier), someday (hider in time), might (qualifier), it (generalizer)

5. pretty much (qualifier), it (generalizer), I used to be (hider in time), suppose (qualifier), I will (hider in time), that stuff (generalizer), if (hider in blaming)

III. Reflection of feelings

A. Compare your reflections of feeling for the client statements on page 94 with these:

1. You're embarrassed about attending Harris High.

2. You're lonely and a little bit desperate for some friendship.

3. You're disappointed with yourself for making a wrong assumption and angry at him for being cold toward you.

4. You're worried about failing some classes and embarrassed that they are in your major.
5. You're really disappointed at not being able to play. It sounds like a little bit of "poor me" or self-pity is creeping in there too.
6. Your drinking behavior has you a little bit worried.

B. Compare your reflections of feeling to those keyed for III-C as well as considering the following analyses of the statements:
   1. Each of the concerns has no apparent ready resolution yet demands action.
   2. The condition seems to be impossible to resolve, so accepting it is an obvious choice. Acceptance is blocked by something—self-pity.
   3. Another situation that requires acceptance. Acceptance has been accomplished.
   4. If I can't or won't tell the thoughts, I must be afraid of what others may think about me for having them.
   5. A common reaction (hooked on TV) but to an obvious extreme; therefore, annoyance is not a strong enough statement of feeling.
   6. The Socratic questioning of obvious content suggests a wish to be told the obvious and desire to not hear the obvious.

C. 1. (b); 2. (a); 3. (d); 4. (c); 5. (a); 6. (d).

IV. Description of situation
   Caution is necessary to avoid the assumption that all of the things in the following segments apply to a person in the situation described or that nothing else applies. These lists are only suggestive of possible dynamics and serve only as an aid in helping the client to explore and share his/her phenomenal space.

   A. You have been in a serious automobile accident that affected your spinal cord in the lumbar region, leaving you paralyzed from the waist down.
      1. Mourning
         Loss of ability

             Feel sorry for self
             Why did it happen to me?

2. Loss of status
   I'm not as good as others.
   I'm not as good as I used to be.
   Focus on handicap and what I can't do instead
      of on remaining abilities: what I can do.
   I can't expect my wife to stay with me now.
   I don't deserve to live in this condition.

3. Need to depend on others, ask for help or tolerance or understanding

4. Anger
   At other driver
   At difficulties
   At God

5. Guilt for being angry or short with spouse, parents, or others who try to help but don't really understand

6. Feeling of isolation
   Nobody understands
   Nobody really cares

7. Embarrassment
   At involuntary tremors or leg movements
   At perceiving the discomfort or condescension of others

8. Sensitive
   To buildings without ramps
   To restrooms without hand bars
   To words like *cripple, handicapped*

9. Overprotection by others: People treat me like I can't do *anything*. I still have lots of ability!

B. After 15 years of fidelity to your spouse, you find yourself caught in an affair with your next-door neighbor.

1. Guilt
   What a terrible thing I've done!
   What kind of a person am I?
   How can I ever make it up to my spouse?
   What will I tell mother?

2. Confusion
   What should I do?
   Should I leave?
   Should I stay?
   Suicide?
   Should I go to the other person?
3. Surprise
   I didn't intend to go that far.
   How did it ever happen?
   I didn't know it would cause so much pain.
   I thought I would handle it better.
4. Frustration
   My spouse seems to want more closeness and reassurance than ever, and from me. How can I be loving and reassuring when I feel so guilty and unworthy?
5. Dislike for myself
6. Rationalization
   It's no big deal. Why is everyone so upset?
7. Remembering mostly good things from the past 15 years that are now in jeopardy because of my unfaithfulness.
8. Sorrow at the thought of losing children, home, status, friends.

C. You are the oldest child in a family with three younger sisters. For two years your father has been engaging you in incestuous activities.
   It must have been my fault.
   I am bad because I didn't stop it.
   I am bad because I enjoyed it.
   Daddy is a bad person; I hate him.
   Daddy is a good person; I love him.
   I wonder if he did the same thing to my sisters.
   Mother didn't believe me at first.
   Mother said I must have seduced him. She thinks it's my fault.
   What will people think of me now?
   I feel so dirty.
   I am no longer desirable as a wife.

> I have committed a grave sin.
>
> I feel sorry for myself.
>
> I'm not such a bad person. I didn't know what was happening.
>
> It's not fair that I should suffer from what he did to me.
>
> I don't want them to take him away.
>
> My sisters need to be protected from him.
>
> Mother should divorce him for doing that.
>
> Why couldn't I have the kind of father that other people have?

D.   At Grange High School you were a student-body officer and a starter on the basketball team. After transferring to Urban Mammoth High School, you refuse to even try out for any sports or activities.

> Overwhelmed
>
> Doubtful of my abilities
>
> Afraid to find out that I'm not good enough
>
> Miss my old routine
>
> Miss my old friends
>
> Upset, maybe angry at having to move
>
> Isolated and fearful
>
> Don't know the expectations of teachers
>
> Need to adjust to new rules
>
> What if people don't like me?
>
> I feel like a country cousin.

E.   You've been separated from your wife and family for 12 months because of a remote work assignment. Next week you will return home.

1.   Joy

> I'm so happy to be going home.
>
> It will be so nice to play with the kids again.
>
> I've been lonely for my wife, and now the long wait is over.
>
> We're going to do so many neat things together.

2.   Hesitation

> Will things be the same?
>
> Will she be happy to see me?

They are so used to getting along without me;
will I be needed? Will I be intruding?

What will my role be in disciplining the kids?

Will our intimate relationship be okay?

Do they resent me for being gone?

3. Resolve

I'm going to make up for all the things we've
missed out on.

Things will be better even than before I left.

4. Regret

I'm not too pleased at some of the things I did
while I was gone.

5. Unsureness

Have my wife or children done things I would
not want them to do? Should I ask or just
assume the best?

F. Your husband has a violent temper, especially when
he has been drinking. He beats you frequently and
sometimes severely. You are at the battered-women's
shelter following one of the more severe beatings.

I hate him.

I love him.

He's a good person.

He's a bad person.

He wouldn't have hit me if I didn't deserve it.

We'll work it out this time. It'll be better.

He's so nice to me when he's not drunk.

I know he didn't mean to hurt me.

I'll never go back.

I want to go back.

What else can I do? Where can I go? Who else
would have me?

I need to be strong for my children's sake.

I could never divorce him. Divorce is bad.

I married him for better or worse.

I'm not a quitter.

Oh, how I hate getting beaten up!

If I had a good job, I could leave him.

G. You're engaged to a person who is of a different race

and religion from yours. Your parents are adamantly opposed to your marrying him/her.

> I love him/her and it doesn't matter what anyone else thinks.
>
> I wonder if it's really wise to marry him/her.
>
> Mom and Dad will get used to the idea.
>
> Sociologists say that the odds are against us.
>
> I never was too much into my church anyway.
>
> He/she'll change to my religion later.
>
> It's hard to go against my parents.
>
> I want them to like me.
>
> Why do they compare me with my older sister/brother?
>
> If I marry him/her I'll never be able to go home again.
>
> Is it really fair to our children?
>
> If kids are loved, that's all that matters, and we'll love our children no matter how they look.
>
> My parents have no right to try to control my life.

H. You are a third-quarter junior, and you are flunking out of school.

> I could do it if I really tried.
>
> Maybe working full time and carrying a full load wasn't too smart.
>
> I can always work on construction or join the army.
>
> I didn't really want to be an engineer anyway.
>
> Dad will really be disappointed.
>
> What a waste of time and money to flunk out after three years.
>
> It wasn't all wasted. I got some good out of college.
>
> Maybe I'm just not smart enough to succeed.
>
> It's the teachers' fault. They didn't give me a chance.
>
> What am I going to do now?

I. Your spouse and two of your three children have just been killed in a fire that destroyed your home.

> I should have; if only I had; they'd be alive now if I had: come home earlier, checked the fire alarms, practiced fire drills.

Why couldn't it have been me instead? I wish I were
    dead.
I must live for my remaining child.
How can I go on without my spouse?
I can't believe this is happening.
Why did it have to happen?
It's not fair.
They were so happy, so full of life.
I'm going to miss them so much.
I must go on!
I've got to be strong!
I hurt so much!
What about the funeral? the insurance settlement?
    the relatives?
I'm so thankful for friends and family.
They just don't understand.
Why are they all looking at me in pity? Go away!
    Leave me alone!
Don't leave me alone! Help me! Hold me!

Chapter 4

ENHANCING SKILLS
General

Therapy is an occurrence that involves at least two people, both of whom are focusing on understanding dynamics within the phenomenal space or life experience of the client. Once an understanding is accomplished, an alteration can be made to produce a solution to existing problems.

There is a dynamic process going on in the mind and/or experience of the client that has two focuses. The first is to explain in an understandable fashion to the therapist just what the conditions are. The second is to produce in the client, an evolving, ever-clearer awareness of those conditions whose appearance gradually sharpens through the process of counseling.

Often this sharpening of understanding involves mulling over, sorting among, or sifting the contents of awareness in a variety of ways. This is referred to as processing the data or contents of consciousness.

Because of individual differences between and among clients, their processing does not always proceed in the same way. The amount of paraphrasing or the relative emphasis on reflection of feeling or nonverbal cues will vary from client to client depending on type or ease of the client's processing. Certainly the quickness or depth in the effective use of description of situation will be a function of client receptiveness to that technique.

There are several skills whose frequency of use or even presence at all in the therapeutic interaction is dependent on client differences in style or ability to process. Their employment will be selective and in accord with objectives of processing.

GUIDELINES FOR PROCESSING

Three general objectives of processing are: (a) increasing the perceptual field of the client, (b) altering the focus from distant and past to the present—here and now, and (c) avoiding certain therapist actions that work against the first two.

It is common for people who seek help to have narrowed their perception so much that they can see only one or two alternatives, neither of which is acceptable or possible. Often there exist other choices that would readily resolve the current difficulty, but since they are not seen, they are, in fact, not choices at all.

Perhaps a simple example of this phenomenon is the experience of approaching a door, pushing on it with the expectation that it will give way to the push, and finding it to be unresponsive to the effort. Because the perception is that the door opens outward, we push again to no avail, look for evidence of its being locked, and perhaps seek another door or stand back in confusion while someone else approaches the door, *pulls* it open, and walks on through.

Increasing the perceptual field pertains to internal as well as external fields. Being aware of emotional needs and responses, of value guides and limits and stress, of abilities and confidences, and of habitual responses and limitations is important in most problem resolutions and is critical in some. This is so important that some entire therapeutic methods are directed toward getting in touch with feelings, value establishment and/or alteration, self-concept building or strengthening, and habit alteration. These special methods will be addressed in chapter 5.

Increasing the external field is concerned mostly with studying and evaluating conditions that are facilitative or inhibitive of problem resolution. It can safely be said that for each client and for each problem there are many more than the two or three options that he/she has been grappling with. In most cases, there exists a myriad of choices ranging from terribly bad to impossibly good and with a whole bunch of midrange choices, any one of which could prove to be entirely satisfactory.

Examples of restricted decision fields would include the person who is just completing college or technical school saying, "If I can't get a job in my area of training, I will have to go on welfare." Another statement in the same situation is "The only good job openings are in locations where I refuse to live." An even more extreme example fits the form of "Either I will be 100 percent successful or I'll commit suicide," or "If she leaves me, I'll just die."

The logic of these two-alternative traps seems as foolish as pushing on the door that must be pulled; however, when faced with the problem and the tensions involved in the decision, objective perception and logical approach to alternatives are difficult to accomplish.

Usually a proper and effective processing of client circumstances requires the counselor to see things from a different frame of reference. The really important frame of reference is the one internal to the client. How does the client see things, feel about things, hear things, value things, approach or avoid things, experience things? It is only from the client's frame of reference that circumstances can be thoroughly understood. It is only based on the client's understanding that successful coping activities can be generated and carried through.

Unfortunately, there is a tendency for many, perhaps most, people to respond to reality as interpreted from an external frame of reference, i.e., father's interpretation, society's interpretation. If I am extremely concerned with how I *should* see things or how I'm told to see them, I can't be very effective at seeing them as they relate to *me*. The therapeutic process usually involves moving from an external frame of reference to the client's internal frame of reference. For example:

> *Client:*   People should be responsible for themselves
> and others. They aren't supposed to treat each
> other so badly.

> *Counselor:* *You* are concerned, maybe angry, at the way
> *you're* being treated.

Words and phrases like "I have to" or "It would be a good idea to" tend to show an external frame of reference and are markedly different from "I want to" or "I choose to." Here is another example of moving from an external to an internal frame of reference by use of a paraphrase:

> *Client:* I really ought to clean up this apartment be-
> fore going to the game.
> (*Note*: Where is the "ought to" coming from?
> Outside of the client, obviously.)
> *Counselor:* You don't much want to be bothered by clean-
> ing right now.

Another simple fact that frequently escapes the client and inexperienced helpers has to do with time. Concerns and feelings are in the present; they exist now. Their antecedents may lie in the past or in the future, but they are now *and* they are here. Understanding and planning for resolution of concerns and aberrant feelings also occur in the present. Often client verbalizations are focused on distant times and places; they talk of then and there. Effective therapeutic dynamics involve moving from then and there to here and now. For example:

> *Client:* My father was always mean to me when I was
> little.
> *Counselor:* You are upset with your father for the way he
> treated you.
> *Or:* You are still bothered by your father's mis-
> treatment of you.

The therapist's role is to explore *with* clients their concerns and feelings and to teach them to be thorough and nondefensive, to own their problems, and to take a responsible and active part in solving them.

There are some things that the therapist generally should avoid doing, things that mostly work against the principles just explained. Six such things to avoid are:

1. Giving personal examples. Generally, personal references are attempts to convey evidence of understanding or examples for solving problems. It is better to paraphrase for understanding and to develop solutions from the client's perspective. The beneficial aspects of self-disclosure in relationship building will come more from honest and caring use of SITE skills than from storytelling.

2. Providing answers to personal questions such as "How old are you?" or "How long since you got your license?" Usually there is an underlying concern that can be paraphrased, such as "You're concerned that I may not be old enough or experienced enough to help you with your problem."

3. Giving advice. Approaches to problem solving are usually followed with more energy, and hence are more likely to succeed, if they are discovered or created by the person using them. A borrowed solution or one pushed on someone frequently is not taken as seriously, and its giver is blamed for subsequent failure: "Your advice didn't work."

The above three are all responses out of the counselor's frame of reference. At best they are harmless, but even so they prevent focus on the client where it must be in order for therapeutic progress to occur.

4. Stating "I know how you feel." Although it's tempting to speak so authoritatively and knowingly, such a statement is basically not true. I don't/can't know how anybody else feels, and to say I do typically invites a challenge to that statement. "I understand" is another invitation to challenge.

5. Asserting the therapist's attitudinal set on the client. It's more productive to let the client lead. If a position on an issue must be presented, care should be taken to present several positions and alternatives in addition to the one preferred by the therapist. If biases need to be stated, they should be clearly labeled as such.

6. Expressing sympathy. If the therapist takes on the client's frame of reference, he/she can only sympathize and hurt with the client; this helps neither person. A good therapist maintains an objective distance.

By focusing on those activities and skills that foster increased client awareness within the client's frame of reference and by avoiding things that detract from those goals, the therapist facilitates direct and efficient progress toward problem resolution. The initiating skills of chapter 2 and the tracking skills of chapter 3 are consistent with these objectives in therapeutic processing. In addition, there are some general process enhancers that form an essential portion of a therapist's repertoire of skills.

GENERAL PROCESS ENHANCERS

There are skills that help the client to become more aware of internal and external conditions, facilitate ventilation, and promote problem definition; they differ slightly from initiating and tracking skills in that they do not fit neatly into a sequence that parallels depth of communication. Some occur rarely; others operate continuously; all enhance the process set in motion by proper use of initiating and tracking skills.

These skills, the general process enhancers, are different also from the theory-specific, goal-directed skills, which tend to be mutually exclusive of each other and therefore are best used each by itself in a theory-pure, therapeutically efficient manner. The specific process enhancers will be described in chapter 5.

The general process enhancers are dealt with under the labels proper use of silence; pacing; physical contact—touch; minimizing interrogation; perception checking; and managing the process. These labels, much the same as the ones used in previous chapters, at present have no universality of meaning. Some will be encountered in presentations on communication, counseling, therapy, human relations, and elsewhere. The reader is cautioned to study the definitions and descriptions that follow in order to understand the behavior and experiences keyed by the labels.

Proper Use of Silence

Even as the artist employs blank spaces and the composer of music accentuates sound by periodic quiet, so too does the therapist use silence in technical and artistic ways. Silence is more than just relief from noise or action; the presence of silence does not indicate absence of productivity.

Silence is unstructured time that has two qualities. One is pressure to fill it. Most people become uncomfortable with silence of more than a few seconds when they are in someone else's company; therefore, therapist silence is a subtle pressure for client talk. Since the client knows most about him/herself and the therapist needs input from the client, therapist silence provides a support for the "You talk, I listen" dynamic of productive therapy.

This is not to say that the interview should include lots of long, awkward silences or that the therapist should never break silences. It does place proper emphasis on client production and disclosure.

A second quality of unstructured time is that of permitting thought, memory, feeling, and/or awareness on the part of the client. Particularly with difficult content or painful disclosure, the therapist needs a well-developed patience. Even in instances where it seems quite obvious what the client wants or intends to say, there is merit in letting him/her say it rather than doing it for the client.

Silence will occur early and frequently in a good therapeutic interaction. Certainly it will appear after each paraphrase, reflection of feeling, description of situation, and virtually every counselor lead or response. The length of the silence probably is a function of the client, who will break the great majority of the silences.

Occasionally a period of silence will be directed by the therapist; e.g., "Now just sit quietly for a time and focus on your feelings." Such use of silence is intended to produce additional insight and data for processing.

Pacing

One technique that can be useful to the therapist in achieving more complete awareness of the client's experience is called pacing. Some therapists employ pacing with all their clients as a primary channel for understanding client experience; others use it selectively for times when they are experiencing difficulty from reliance on their customary techniques. Proponents of one theoretical approach contend that pacing and its companion technique, mirroring, are integral to effective therapy. From that source, pacing and mirroring are defined in this manner:

> To the extent that you can match another person's behavior, both verbally and non-verbally, you will be pacing their experience. Mirroring is the essence of what most people call rapport. . . . You can mirror the other person's predicates and syntax, body posture, breathing, voice tone and tempo, facial expression, eye blinks, etc. (Bandler & Grinder, 1979, p. 79)

Because pacing is not universally accepted as critical to all therapy yet appears to be effective in enhancing the tracking process, it is included here, perhaps in an altered form, as a general process enhancer.

Much the same way that marching in step with others in a precision drill team produces a feeling of togetherness and unity of experience, so too does "breathing" in step or "sitting" in step or matching volume or speed of talking produce for the therapist some additional insight into the client's state of being.

There is an important caution to be noted here. Body posture, breathing rhythm, voice volume and speed are not necessarily universal correlates to the same experience. What the counselor achieves by shallow and rapid breathing is access to his/her own past experiences that fit with that breathing pattern. This provides a hint to what the client may be experiencing; this hint can then be verified. The caution is against believing that the therapist's copy of the client's behavior provides direct access to the client's experience. In the same manner that specific words do not always correspond to identical meanings for different people, specific behavioral manifestations do not signify the same experience for everyone.

The primary value in pacing is the provision of suggestive data that can be verified by mirroring actions back to the client, formalizing of nonverbal cues brought to awareness by pacing,

and paraphrasing messages or reflecting feelings that are cued
by the pacing process.

Physical Contact — Touch

Some specialized therapies use extensive physical contact on
the theoretical basis that a person's mental or emotional
condition affects the body and that direct manipulation of the
body will in turn have a positive effect on the emotional or mental state (Lowen, 1975). For centuries philosophers have debated
whether people are dualistic (mind-body or spirit-body) or monistic and thoroughly integrated (Lowen, 1975, Reich, 1970).

Such underpinnings may be important for use of physical
contact for achieving a specific therapeutic goal. For purposes of
forming a therapeutic relationship and for initiating, tracking,
and processing of client information, the theoretical issues are
not of primary importance. Pragmatically, selective use of physical touch provides enhancement for the early stages of therapy.

Parenthetically, it should be stated that there appear to
be rather great individual differences between and among clients and therapists relative to the effects of touch. On one extreme, touch can be interpreted by the client as a violation of
self, thereby producing a personal resistance to counseling. On
the other hand, some clients seem to require touch in order to
risk any personal affect in a relationship. Some counselors are so
uncomfortable with touching that to do so would be interpreted
as artificial and "techniquey"; others communicate quite naturally and genuinely through physical contact.

Certain agencies and some social groups prohibit or dis-
courage touch, fearing accusations of legal or moral infractions.
Of course some physical contact can be inappropriate, counterproductive, and even harmful to therapy. The code of ethics of
the American Psychological Association treats selfish manipulation of any kind, including touch, as improper and unethical. It
specifically mentions sexual relationships between therapist and
client as being unethical.

There are many variables in the process of physical touch as
part of a realtionship. Like fire, it has the potential of enhance-

ment or destruction, depending on how it is used. To use touch carelessly is certainly wrong; to avoid its use when appropriate and therapeutic also may be wrong (Mintz, 1969).

In addition to being careful and timely with touch, the manner of touching is important. The variations are numerous and difficult to define; however, here are three continua for consideration: (a) intensity—soft versus hard, (b) speed—slow versus fast, and (c) quality—supportive versus seductive or manipulative.

Therapist needs and style must be constantly monitored. "Whose needs are being served at this time?" and even if the client's, "Are those needs appropriately served in a professional, therapeutic manner?" are two questions that are important to all counseling activities and especially to those involving physical contact. A third question that serves as a selective control in this regard is "What is the probability of my touch being misinterpreted by my client?"

For clients who are not repulsed by touch, the following uses appear to be safe and warranted:

1. On introduction—a handshake or similar social amenity.
2. At the beginning of each successive interview.
3. Holding hand(s) or a hug as a signal to release pent-up affect; i.e., as an invitation to cry.
4. For reassurance and support after a particularly difficult disclosure.
5. At the end of sessions.
6. Occasionally to dramatize obvious body tension, usually accompanying formalization of nonverbal cues.

Probably a good rule for beginning therapists is "Too little touch is better than too much." Being cautious is good, but risking a touch response when it "feels" right will allow the therapist to develop a sensitive and powerful therapeutic skill. In many ways psychotherapy is like an advanced art form. Much can be learned from observing a skilled therapist; perhaps this is true in the area of physical touch more than with any other therapeutic skill.

Minimizing Interrogation

The most frequent mistake of neophyte counselors is reliance on interrogative leads. This is such a problem that it merits the only negatively stated one of the sequential initiating, tracking, and enhancing skills.

Broadly interpreted, the precaution against interrogation could be stated, "Don't ask questions." Some kinds of questions can be very helpful and would certainly be appropriate in therapy. Because there is a tendency for inexperienced therapists to rely too heavily on questions, there is merit in the limiting of all kinds of interrogative leads.

More specifically, the intent of this general process enhancer is to avoid questions that can be answered by a one- or few-word response, and particularly yes or no. These are called closed questions.

The use of the word *interrogation* in this section refers to use of closed questions. The "grilling" of a criminal suspect by an overzealous detective provides the stereotype for interrogation as used here.

Why is interrogation so bad? First, it is inefficient. If there are 100 possible questions, the odds of asking the important one is only 1 in 100. Even if the important question is asked, it can receive a partially true or untrue reply.

Second, and more important, interrogative interaction gives the client the power and the therapist the responsibility. The counselor must do all the work with relatively little direction from the client. It requires the client to know what is going on within him/herself and to understand the therapist's framework on which the questions are based. If clients could do this, they would have little or no need for counselors.

Avoiding interrogation reinforces the use of indirect leads, paraphrases, and other more powerful techniques.

Perception Checking

Virtually all of the initiating and tracking skills permit the therapist to form impressions or perceptions of a client's condition. Almost all replies by the client to such skills permit the therapist to test, "check," validate his/her perceptions. Perception checking as a technique, however, refers to a special use and modification of those skills.

Whenever the therapist precedes or follows a paraphrase, reflection of feeling, description of situation, and so on with one of the following phrases or its equivalent, the therapist is perception checking:

> "Tell me if I'm right."
> "Let's see if I'm understanding correctly."
> "Correct me if I'm wrong."
> "Is this the way you see it?"
> "Am I right?"
> "Have I got it down accurately?"
> "Am I seeing it right?"

The effect of such therapist statements is to slow the process, invite an intellectual response from the client by asking the client to evaluate the therapist's statement, and produce an interrogative lead. If the perception check is accurate or reasonably close, the client may well reply, "Yes" or "That's right." If inaccurate, the client can change the interaction dramatically by simply saying, "No" or "You don't understand." Usually, however, the client will attempt to make a clarification and correct the misunderstanding of the therapist.

Because of the slowing, stopping, or confounding of process resulting from its use, perception checking should be employed rarely and only in those situations that clearly call for it, primarily when the client is markedly defensive and not receptive to the usually more effective techniques. The perception check in this case tends to soften the impact of the tracking skill.

For example, defensiveness or resistance that signals use of perception checking may approximate this:

> *Client:* Sometimes I get so mad at him I could just pound him to little pieces.
> *Counselor:* You get extremely angry at him.
> *Client:* Well, no! Not *extremely* angry. I mean I don't really want to kill him, or anything like that.

Although it seems a little nonsensical, a change to perception checking usually results in a smoother process, like this:

> *Counselor:*   Let me see if I've got this right. You really get
>   extremely angry at him.
> *Client:*   Yes. That's right. I'm afraid that I might seriously hurt him someday.

In addition to managing resistance, perception checking can be used to cause the client to rehearse intellectually what he/she has been saying, to confront an awareness of his/her conditions, and to own them. This promotes an integration of affect, intellect, and history for the client and usually leads well into a personal analysis and sorting of conditions and their meanings. Used in this way, perception checking is a useful device.

Managing the Process

If a therapist is to be effective, he/she must be expert at managing the therapeutic process. Clients do not know how to be good clients; they must be shown. They come to be "counseled" or helped or fixed or whatever. Many believe that they are coming to receive "the answer" or to be enlightened, guru style.

The therapist, through management of process, is responsible for making things happen that result in an improved state for the client. All of the techniques described thus far are important in properly managing the process.

Obviously engaging in interrogation, chitchat, gossip, or any other nontherapeutic interaction constitutes mismanagement of process. Some questions help to evaluate whether or not the interaction is on track:

1. Who's doing most of the talking?
2. Who's in control of the process?
3. Is there lots of paraphrasing of messages?
4. Is interrogation absent or minimal?
5. Are therapist responses consistent with or appropriate to the state of the client?

The client should be talking most, with the counselor doing the tracking and processing from a position of control. Lots of paraphrasing and little interrogation typically mark a good interaction.

It is important to make a distinction between content control and process control. Because the content to be dealt with exists in client phenomenal space, the client is in the best position to manage its disclosure. If talking about certain content is too threatening, the client will typically resist disclosing it.

Although it may be possible for a therapist to force or manipulate clients into saying things against their preference, it is much more advisable to use process management techniques to gently invite progressively deeper disclosures and to process them thoroughly.

Through judicious and skilled use of the SITE skills the therapist controls the process: who's talking most and at what level of the funnel, with continual focus on the client's phenomenal space. The client will exercise control over how much, from what area, and the pace of work within his/her space.

Gazda, Asbury, Balzer, Childers, & Walters (1977) have developed a scale for evaluating effectiveness of counselor responses. Basically, a technically accurate use of the SITE skills will produce consistently a moderately therapeutic performance on their scale. To go beyond being moderately therapeutic requires lots of practice, feedback, and the development of multichannel monitoring and understanding to an almost intuitive level. The therapist becomes an intensely functioning therapeutic instrument.

Not everyone can be expected to achieve excellence in managing the therapeutic process. Fortunately, there are applications of the skills in many settings that do not require extremely high levels of therapeutic performance. For those who have the talent, training, and perseverance necessary to be truly therapeutic, theirs is a unique experience of being.

Summary

Objectives of therapeutic processing include increasing both the internal and external perceptual fields of the client. To accomplish this it is recommended that processing be rooted in the clients' conditions as seen by them.

Movement of attention from data and experiences that happened in distant times and places to events and experiences in the present is necessary for resolving problems that may have originated elsewhere but must be understood and resolved here and now.

Some counterproductive things to avoid are therapist reference to personal experiences, answers to personal data questions, giving advice, saying "I know how you feel," stating personal values or biases, and giving sympathy.

There are some skills that work in a general sense to enhance the therapeutic process. Some show up frequently in most therapy sessions; others receive selective use at appropriate times. These general process enhancers are labeled proper use of silence; pacing; physical contact—touch; minimizing interrogation; perception checking; and managing the process. Practical and sensitive use of all of the SITE skills will produce a truly therapeutic experience.

EXERCISES

I.   Perception check
 A.   Write a perception check for each of the client statements in exercises I-Al and III-B of the more difficult exercises for chapter 3, pages 94–101.
 B.   From the following list select responses that are perception checks:
  1.   You feel angry at him for doing that!
  2.   You believe that he cheated you; am I right?
  3.   Now is this how it is? He withdrew money from your joint account without you knowing?
  4.   Some days it just doesn't pay to get out of bed.
  5.   I have this vision of you blindly consenting to his request. How does it match with reality?
  6.   He doesn't admit to doing anything wrong?

II. Silence
 Answer the following questions:
 A.   What are the two qualities of unstructured time?

B.   At what times or under what conditions does silence occur in a good therapeutic session?

C.   What are three possible interpretations for silence on the part of the client?

III.   Pacing

Describe four ways of pacing a client.

IV.   Physical contact—touch

A.   Imagine yourself as a therapist. In what ways and under what conditions would you comfortably touch a(n):

1.   child, five years of age?

2.   prostitute who is trying to reform?

3.   cancer patient, male, middle-aged?

4.   thirty-year-old female amputee?

5.   each of the above if Mexican-American, Black, Native American?

6.   elderly man prone to bowel and bladder incontinence?

B.   What three questions are helpful guidelines for proper use of therapeutic touch?

V.   Minimizing interrogation

A.   Try to spend one entire day without asking a question that can be answered with one or two words.

B.   Substitute an indirect lead for each of the following questions:

1.   How old are you?

2.   Why are you here?

3.   Have you tried asking for a loan?

4.   Did your mother love you?

5.   Are you really depressed?

VI.   Managing the process

List the five questions that are useful in evaluating the counseling process.

VII.   Applications

For the following situations write three counselor actions that would be acceptable and probably useful. Do not limit yourself to chapter 4 skills.

A.   Sally comes from an extremely conservative, rigid home environment. She has been complaining about an empty feeling deep inside. She starts to cry softly.

B. Harry is relating in a matter-of-fact way how he is 2 weeks behind schedule and will lose his job if he doesn't catch up quickly. Although his voice is calm, his foot is tapping quite rapidly, and there is a half-smile on his face.

Responses for Comparison

I. Perception Check
    A. (I-A, chapter 3, page 94)
        1. Is it true that you're not very proud of your actions during school?
        2. Correct me if I'm wrong; you are emotionally isolated and don't know what to do about it.
        3. You assumed too much, and now you have alienated him; is that right?
        4. Let's see if I'm understanding correctly; the studying you do while you're fresh is producing better results than what you put off till last?
        5. What I'm hearing is you trying hard to talk yourself out of the disappointment you're feeling; how close to right am I?
        6. How does this fit? Your drinking is causing you some concern. Maybe you aren't handling it as well as you'd like to believe.
    B. (III-B, chapter 3, page 101)
        1. Let's see if I've got it; you feel trapped and sort of panicky?
        2. Am I right that it's hard not to feel sorry for yourself?
        3. Is this the way you see it: you miss him but still get happiness from his memory?
        4. Correct me if I'm wrong, but it's really scary to have such thoughts; you're not sure of your sanity.
        5. You're pretty well disgusted with yourself over this TV habit; is that right?
        6. What you're feeling is sorrow and shame for what you did; am I correct?
    C. Numbers 2, 3, and 5 are perception checks.

II. Silence
    A. Pressure to fill it and permission to think, feel, remember, or increase awareness.
    B. Early and frequently; after each paraphrase, reflection of feeling, description of situation, almost all counselor leads or responses; occasionally directed by the therapist.
    C. Confusion; management of emotion; e.g., holding back tears, afraid to answer; resistance; composing or rehearsing a response.

        There are other reasons that are evident sometimes from the context in which silence occurs. It is permissible and appropriate to ask a client what he/she is being silent about or to paraphrase from the cues that are present.

III. Pacing
    breathing in the same rhythm as client
    assuming the same posture
    speaking at the same speed
    speaking with the same volume
    making the same gestures
    looking in the same direction
    using some of the same key words in the same way

IV. Physical contact—touch
    A. Analyze your imaginary encounters with the make-believe clients relative to whether you varied your touch patterns out of personal concern (for yourself) or out of concern for each of them. Because there are so many variables involved, it is impossible to describe a specific, always correct manner of touch for these examples.
    B. Whose needs are being served at this time?

        Are those needs appropriately served in a professional, therapeutic relationship?

        What is the probability of my touch being misinterpreted by my client?

V. Minimizing interrogation
    A. This is just an exercise in avoiding interrogation. It is not a prescription for regular behavior. There are lots of occasions when interrogation is appropriate

and efficient. It is possible, however, to substitute indirect leads for many instances of habitual interrogation.

B. 1. Tell me about yourself.
Give me some personal data.
Describe yourself to me.

2. Share with me your reasons for coming.
What events led to your being here?

3. What things have you already tried in working on this problem?
Describe for me what you have already done.
What options have you considered?

4. Tell me about your childhood.
Describe your family relationship.
Tell me how you and your mother got along.
Give me some examples of how you related with your parents.

5. Tell me how you arrived at your present condition.
What symptoms or experiences cause you to believe you're depressed?

VI. Managing the process
Learning to manage the process requires lots of experience and cannot be neatly expressed in a written exercise. The following are criteria for evaluating good management:

A. Who's doing most of the talking?

B. Who's in control of the process?

C. Is there lots of paraphrasing of messages?

D. Is interrogation absent or minimal?

E. Are therapist responses consistent with or appropriate to the cognitive, affective, and behavioral state of the client?

VII. Applications

A. 1. Nothing

2. Hand her a tissue and say, "It's okay to cry."

3. Pace her posture and expression.

4. Reflect feeling.

5. Describe situation; maybe use an analogy.

  6. Take hold of her hand(s) slowly and not too firmly.

B. 1. Formalize the nonverbal inconsistency with the verbal content.

  2. Pace the foot tapping and mirror it back in exaggerated form.

  3. Reflect feeling of tension.

  4. Paraphrase message.

  5. Silence.

  6. Perception-check the urgency expressed by the tapping foot and words about losing his job.

Chapter 5

ENHANCING SKILLS
Specific

Appropriate and effective use of the SITE skills described in the previous chapters results in the establishment of a communication process, a therapeutic relationship, and clarification of client style and circumstance. Once these are accomplished, therapy of a more problem-specific and style-specific nature can be started.

It is a common error for nonprofessional counselors to pursue actively their solutions to what they think is the client's problem. The SITE skill approach helps counselors to postpone solution strategies long enough to be sure of the problems and style of the client. The change from the clarification phase to the alteration phase is a time when therapists can become much more active and/or directive in teaching clients new approaches to remedying their situations.

Parenthetically, it is important to point out that highly proficient, experienced therapists may move through the SITE sequence very rapidly and with surprising perceptiveness. Observers, and even clients themselves, often say, "How did you know?" or "Where did you get that awareness?" It is this rapid and efficient early-stage performance that obscures the commonality of therapists from different "schools" or theoretical identities. No one pays a lot of attention to foundations when the superstructures are rich and varied. It may have been the common nature of therapeutic foundations that led Hans Strupp (1968) to say, "No single school of therapy has a monopoly on the truth, and when all is said and done we shall probably find that their basic similarities are more impressive than their alleged differences" (p. 97).

Having identified client style and circumstance, the obvious next step is to institute an action that will resolve circumstantial problems in the most effective manner. The techniques to be applied will be those that most closely apply to the particular client problem and style in focus at the time. They can be said to be *specific* to the process at hand, hence the label, specific process enhancers.

From analysis of many theories of or approaches to counseling, two aspects of each can be seen. The first is that each contains elements, particularly in the early stages of use, which are similar to elements in other approaches. This observation may be unacceptable to proponents of some models and it may more nearly fit some than others; however, the observed or inferred commonality is the basis for the synthesis of initiating, tracking, and enhancing procedures called SITE skills.

The second aspect seen in analysis of counseling models is that each has a focus and/or techniques that differentiates it from the others. Each does one specific thing better than the others. It is this unique function that is referred to as a specific process enhancer.

When progress in therapy reaches a point at which one or more identifiable problems or deficiencies exist, the decision can be made as to which set of specific techniques will address the specific dynamics at hand.

Therapists who are bound, by ignorance or devotion, to a single counseling model have no decision. They must try to adapt their only approach to all client styles and problems or refer clients elsewhere. The outcomes of such a practice occasionally include helping a person feel accepting of thoughts or actions that are self-defeating, creating a belief that actions that run counter to the client's history and social structure are in fact

okay and need no alteration, and altering behavioral manifestations without regard for emotional or cognitive positions. These
mistakes of therapy are, respectively, attempts to solve behavioral problems by affective methods, behavioral problems by
cognitive methods, and emotional or cognitive problems by
behavioral methods. This will become clearer in the following
sections.

Two other options, other than being a strict disciple of
method, are available. The first is that of eclecticism. Dimond,
Havens, & Jones (1978) say, "it is safe to conclude that most
psychotherapists perceive their practice as embodying some aspects of an eclectic model" (p. 239). They proceed to outline
their preference for an improved, prescriptive eclecticism: "The
concept of prescriptive eclecticism in psychotherapy is an effort
to integrate the ideas, concepts, and techniques of many
psychotherapists into a broad framework that permits and facilitates the development of patient-specific treatment strategies"
(p. 239).

Prescriptive eclecticism addresses the difficulties of discipleship by removing the therapist from a philosophical or theoretical base in order to justify the use of techniques from many of
them. "A basic postulate of prescriptive psychotherapy is that
practitioners pay total allegiance to no single theory of personality and yet accept useful information from all of them"
(Dimond, Havens, & Jones, 1978, p. 241). The broad framework
of eclecticism has some of the same characteristics of the philosophy of pragmatism. Simply stated, whatever works, works; so
use it. The major criticism of eclecticism is that it employs
techniques out of context, and it is the context that makes them
work.

It may be that many successful eclectics are not really eclectic at all. They succeed by using a variety of techniques alter-
nately within the theoretical framework. This is the third, and
preferable, approach to therapy for counselors who wish to
serve a variety of clients. The term *integrationist* identifies it as
different from disciple or eclectic.

Not bound exclusively by a single theoretical framework,
the responsive therapist (integrationist) works to ascertain the
unique problem and style to be addressed and then becomes

"bound to" the appropriate theory, conceptualizations, and methods. In other words, when the problem is behavioral, the therapist becomes a behaviorist, and so on. There is more than a semantic difference between "integrating ideas, concepts, and techniques of many psychotherapists into a broad framework" (Dimond, Havens, & Jones, 1978, p. 239) and an approach that requires knowledge of several therapies and application of them in their respective theoretical contexts.

Perhaps "what works" applies to both eclectic and responsive therapies because it gets used in the appropriate context. It seems to be a safer and more expedient route to approach the training for and conduct of therapy from a definitive and denotative framework that prescribes learning and application of techniques in their correct theoretical context.

The following sections provide support for this assertion as well as descriptions of a variety of specific process enhancers.

INTERNAL CONGRUENCE: AN ANALOG FOR THE GOAL OF THERAPY

To aid in differentiating the various approaches to therapy this section will present an analogy from geometry to positive mental health, which in turn can be seen as a global end point to therapy.

In the study of geometry the term *congruence* refers to the state of exact correspondence between two figures when they are superimposed, particularly pertaining to two triangles having equal legs and equal angles. The three triangles in Figure 5-1 are congruent because superimposition of the three would leave no part of any one hanging over or protruding from the others.

The nature of personality is often broken down into several component parts. A fairly common division includes (a) the intellectual, thinking, or cognitive part of a person's experience; (b) the feeling, emotional, or affective part; and (c) the active, doing, or behavioral part. Some people might wish to include a sensing or experiencing part, and others would include a spiritual part. For our purposes, consideration of the first three— cognitive, affective, and behavioral—will suffice. Albert Ellis

(1968) describes a similar viewpoint in differentiating treatment modalities into the categories of perceptual-cognitive, emotional and motivational, and motor and habituation.

If the previous three triangles are labeled cognitive, affective, and behavioral, a visual definition of positive mental health or adjustment can be achieved (Figure 5-2). When the cognitive, affective, and behavioral components of personality are in a state of exact correspondence or balance, congruent, a state of positive mental health exists.

Some simple examples of incongruence will help focus the analogy. A hypothetical businessman is heard to say that honesty is the best policy—treat people fairly, and they will reciprocate. In his business dealings, however, he takes *every* advantage to increase profit, often at the expense of others. His triangles might look like those in Figure 5-3. To maintain his stability, he would resort to selective perception of his own actions, denial, or rationalization.

Another hypothetical case is the college coed who claims to be liberated from the shackles of her parents' "Victorian value system" and yet lives in very strict accordance with her childhood conditioning (see Figure 5-4) or else experiences tremendous guilt for relatively minor infractions (see Figure 5-5).

Therapy in this latter case could well be directed at chang-

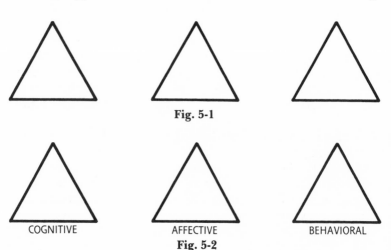

Fig. 5-1

COGNITIVE   AFFECTIVE   BEHAVIORAL
                   Fig. 5-2

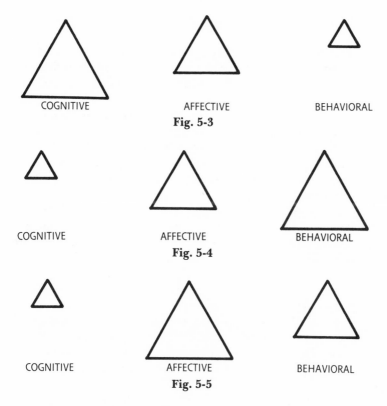

COGNITIVE   AFFECTIVE   BEHAVIORAL
                   Fig. 5-3

COGNITIVE   AFFECTIVE   BEHAVIORAL
                   Fig. 5-4

COGNITIVE   AFFECTIVE   BEHAVIORAL
                   Fig. 5-5

ing her cognitive experience so as to admit considerable constraints from childhood training. It could focus on the emotional discomforts resulting from "transgressions." Her behavior could be the focus of therapy to bring it in line with either or both of the other components. She would be considered to be congruent and adjusted when the three components are balanced; i.e., when she thinks liberation, acts liberated, and feels okay about herself and her actions, or when she acts constrained, realizes the constraints, and accepts her condition with good feelings.

Obviously, the approaches used in therapeutically altering a person's adjustment will have varying effectiveness and results, depending on which component they affect and which component is incongruent.

CLIENT STYLES

The same analogy can be used to illustrate contrasts among clients. Some clients seem to be very much controlled or directed by their cognitive nature. For them, an okay state is synonymous with understanding.

There are two particular concerns relative to dealing with a "thinker." The first is that a method which focuses on cognitive skills will be most readily accepted by the client. To the extent that his/her problem can be resolved through the cognitive access, an intellectual approach will be most effective.

The second concern is an awareness that "thinkers" often ignore feelings. Some are so practiced at ignoring their feeling nature that they are not, cannot, be aware of it. For people like this, whose problems involve lack of feeling integration or are primarily emotional disturbances, the cognitive access will produce, at best, an awareness or explanation but not a resolution of the problem. For them the treatment of choice probably would be an affective access, even though it would be difficult.

It should be realized that a simplistic model such as this is most useful to illustrate and contrast tendencies. The "types" included here are not exclusive or pure, and there are many people who fall between types or who seem to be a combination of two or more types.

A second group of clients are those who seem to be led by their emotions. They act or react intuitively and validate their actions relative to how they feel. Many of these people find themselves in long-term difficulty because feelings are immediate and transitory, working well as guidelines for the present but not being very reliable relative to the future. The easiest therapeutic access is through the affect, but as previously discussed, the easiest is not always the best.

The third group, obviously, are the "behavers." People in this group appear to be controlled by external conditions. They do what the situation demands. To a certain extent it could be said that their lives run them, rather than the other way around. If a person is miscued by his environment, the obvious corrective is to reprogram the reaction to that cue. For these people behavioral access is easier and quicker; but again, caution must be exercised to avoid applying a behavioral cure to an affective or cognitive problem.

There is an apparent overlap or interaction among the three personality components within each person. Sometimes feelings and actions are changed as a result of changing thoughts. Likewise, thoughts and actions may be altered following an affective conversion, and emotional and thought responses may fall into line with behavioral alterations. This is the expectation of some theorists. Albert Ellis (1969) says that his form of therapy "unusually stresses the cognitive aspect of human disturbance, but also importantly deals with its emotive and behavioral aspects" (p. 83).

There is little evidence to support the assertion that the unattended personality components always will come around automatically. A strategy that permits the most direct approach to changing the status of the least congruent component seems to be a better choice.

Before moving to the dynamics of an integrated model, it should be pointed out that the congruence model is a logical analogy for showing that differences in client styles exist. There are no organized data to support an empirical differentiation of clients to promote access by cognitive, affective, and behavioral means. On the other hand, because empirical research data do not exist does not mean that there is no validity in the model.

Bandler and Grinder (1975, 1976, 1979) have proposed another dimensional system for client types and strategies for communication access. Their system postulates a preference in some people to experience visually, others to favor aural representation of experience, and still for others a kinesthetic or tactile mode. Awareness by therapist and client is enhanced or facilitated when the therapist can identify and employ the client's preferred mode of experiencing.

Some work has been done in contrasting field-dependent and field-independent personalities, with some obvious implications for therapist-client selection (Silverman, 1967).

Suffice it to say for now that the type or style of client is an important variable in therapy that needs to be accounted for in the selection of therapeutic strategy.

Application of Appropriate Intervention Method

Included in this section are a differentiation of methods by way of the congruence model, a brief description of several specific enhancing skill systems (methods), and some consideration concerning selection of method.

The descriptions of methods are intended to be brief introductions to the method and explanation as to how they fit into a larger, integrated approach. No attempt is made to provide definitive or comprehensive explanations of the methods. The reader is encouraged to seek out and study in depth several representative methods from each section.

It doesn't take long in the study of any therapeutic method to encounter an attempt to define that particular method further by contrasting it with others. Implicit in this approach, although not always intentional, is the presumption that this is the better, best, or only way to be a successful therapist. Such a conclusion usually follows logically from the theorist's premises about the nature of people. Albert Bandura (1974) skillfully describes the fallacy of this approach. "What we believe man to be affects which aspects of human functioning we study most. Premises thus delimit research and are, in turn, shaped by it" (p. 859). In generalizing, it could be said that a therapist's beliefs about people limit his approach to intervention, and the results of his attempts to intervene further refine his basic beliefs. This is graphically shown in Figures 5-6, 5-7, and 5-8.

An eclectic therapist would most likely favor one of the three emphases but select some methodology from the others to "increase" his/her effectiveness.

The preferred stance for therapists, as espoused by this

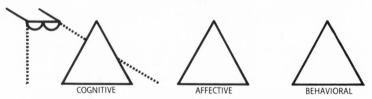

COGNITIVE   AFFECTIVE   BEHAVIORAL

Figure 5-6. Viewpoint of a theorist who believes people are predominantly thought-directed.

Figure 5-7. **Viewpoint of a theorist who believes that people are directed and most in line with their "flow of potential" through affect.**

book, is based on the notion that people are either simultaneously cognitive-affective-behavioral creatures, that there are some clients who will be predominantly cognitive or affective or behavioral, or that people are really a combination of all three but have learned to deal with their reality by habitual reliance on one of the three. This accounts for different styles of people, supports explanations that justify treatment of a client with one particular style by use of an alternate access, and explains why selective, intact approaches are better than eclectic ones.

The wisdom of systematic use of the SITE skills is readily apparent in consideration of the diverse natures and styles of clients. Careful, systematic processing is necessary for the responsive therapist who espouses a broad view that allows the client to define himself. The viewpoint of the responsive therapist would be pictured as in Figure 5-9. This viewpoint removes therapists from the difficult position of deciding which of all the theories is "true" but places them in another dilemma; namely, since all are "true" for some people, in order to be consistently effective,

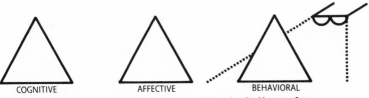

Figure 5-8. **Viewpoint of a theorist who believes that people are controlled by their environment in some form of stimulus-response contingency.**

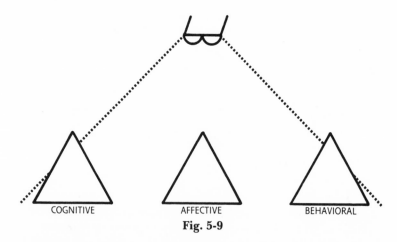

Fig. 5-9

therapists must learn many or all approaches. For the beginning therapist one training strategy would be to learn thoroughly one theoretical approach from each of the emphases: cognitive, affective, behavioral.

GENERAL ENHANCEMENTS: A SPECIAL CASE

The congruence model is very useful in highlighting portions of a person's nature and demonstrating how styles differ and how varying degrees of incongruity or instability occur in maladjustment. Presumably, once a problem is determined to exist in one part (say, cognitive), a strategy can be used that will address that part (say, logic or reasoning or provision of data).

Sometimes there is inconsistency within the subparts. The term *confusion* is used to indicate the presence of two or more competing ideas of somewhat equal veracity. Ambivalence refers to the presence of two incompatible feelings; *contradiction, vacillation, inconsistency* are terms used to describe verbal or motor behavior of a competing or contradictory nature.

The word *psychodynamics* is used to indicate the presence of and relationships among these various subparts of personality. There are references in literature that document the awareness of and problematic nature of duplicity of personality. Two well-known examples from literature follow.

First is a quotation from the fictional Dr. Henry Jekyll:

> I was in no sense a hypocrite; both sides of me were in dead earnest; I was no more myself when I laid aside restraint and plunged in shame, than when I laboured in the eye of day, at the furtherance of knowledge or the relief of sorrow and suffering. And it chanced that the direction of my scientific studies, which led wholly towards the mystic and transcendental, reacted and shed a strong light on this consciousness of the perennial war among my members. With every day, and from both sides of my intelligence, the moral and the intellectual, I thus drew steadily nearer to that truth by whose partial discovery I have been doomed to such a dreadful shipwreck: that man is not truly one, but truly two. I say two, because the state of my own knowledge does not pass beyond that point. Others will follow; others will outstrip me on the same lines; and I hazard the guess that man will be ultimately known for a mere polity of multifarious, incongruous and independent denizens. It was on the moral side, and in my own person, that I learned to recognise the thorough and primitive duality of man; I saw that, of the two natures that contended in the field of my consciousness, even if I could rightly be said to be either, it was only because I was radically both; and from an early date, even before the course of my scientific discoveries had begun to suggest the most naked possibility of such a miracle, I had learned to dwell with pleasure, as a beloved daydream, on the thought of the separation of these elements. If each, I told myself, could but be housed in separate identities, life would be relieved of all that was unbearable; the unjust might go his way, delivered from the aspirations and remorse of his more upright twin; and the just could walk steadfastly and securely on his upward path, doing the good things in which he found his pleasure, and no longer exposed to disgrace and penitence by the hands of this extraneous evil. (Stevenson, pp. 192–193)

The second is quoted from the Christian Apostle Paul in a letter to the people of Rome. "For the good that I would I do not: but the evil which I would not, that I do" (Romans 7:19).

Sigmund Freud separated the personality into id, ego, and superego. He developed a personality theory, a developmental theory, and a therapy model on the dynamics of those constructs. Both the Freudian model and that of Eric Berne, transactional analysis, focus on understanding as the means to therapeutic growth; Berne will be discussed in the section on cognitive models. Even though their focus of therapy is cognitive, their models incorporate intrapsychic (within personality) forces.

Drawing from Dr. Jekyll's quotation, people "will be ultimately known for a mere polity of multifarious, incongruous and independent denizens," it might be postulated that group therapy should be used on each individual client. The analogy of the committee within each of us and its difficulty in reaching consensus is appropriate in this context.

Using Figure 5-8, each of the three subparts can be divided into two, four, or many parts (see Figure 5-10). Concepts and beliefs of competence/incompetence, worthwhile/worthless, strong/weak can exist side by side in the cognitive space. Likewise, eager and afraid may coexist in the affect, feast and diet in the behavioral area.

There is one theoretical model, Gestalt therapy, that is easily confused with other models as specific process enhancers. To the extent that the Gestalt approaches intend to bring a client to

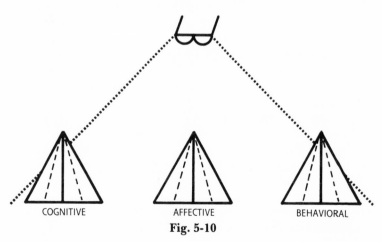

COGNITIVE   AFFECTIVE   BEHAVIORAL

Fig. 5-10

full awareness of his/her unique being and stream of conscious-ness, to accept and go with their flow, it can be considered to be a focused and specific process enhancer. The techniques of Ge-stalt, however, particularly as expressed by William Passons (1975), appear to be general process enhancers that particularly give access to the psychodynamics of intrapsychic entities. A brief focus on Gestalt therapy will provide clarification of this point.

GESTALT THERAPY

Some caution is necessary in properly differentiating Ge-stalt therapy from the slightly related, but markedly different, Gestalt school of psychology.

Around the turn of the century (late 1890s and well into the 1900s) psychology was evolving on several theoretical fronts (Woodworth & Sheehan, 1964). Clinical work was dominated by Freud and psychoanalysis. "Scientific psychology" in America was a combination of behaviorism, with its reductionistic pref-erence for isolating deterministic elements of behavior; struc-turalism and a similarly reductionistic quest for the elements of experience; and functionalism, with its focus on specifics of ap-plication. Gestalt psychology grew largely from European phi-losophy, mostly Germanic, and existed strongly as an antireduc-tionist force; the dictum "the whole is greater than the sum of its parts" reflects the Gestalt belief in the embeddedness of behav-ior and effects of surroundings or context on the "figure" or fo-cus of study. Early Gestalt psychologists were very much in-volved in the study of perception.

Modern-day Gestalt therapy was popularized by Frederick Perls (1969). Its similarity to the earlier Gestalt psychology is su-perficial but probably worth describing. Both took a lot of initial definition and popularity as a reaction against behaviorism and behavioristic methods; both have an emphasis on perception, the school focusing primarily on perceptual processing of visual inputs and insight as a process of perceptual sorting, and the therapy emphasizing awareness of conditions primarily kines-thetic and imaginal. The school could be said to focus on space outside the body, whereas the therapy is concerned with inner space. Both attracted many disciples, and in the case of Gestalt therapy their fervor caused them to label many techniques as Gestalt that historically preceded the movement (see Passons, 1975).

Modern-day Gestalt therapy fits well within the broader rubric of humanistic psychology. It postulates an innate striving on the part of humans, plants, and animals toward self-actualization (Perls, 1969). There is, however, no universal hierarchy of needs, so individuals influence their own status in unique ways. An individual is not separate from his/her environment and thus is a participant in an ongoing flow of dynamic forces. Actualization is a process of "going with the flow," willingly, because of a global awareness of the forces in the flow and the individual's relationship to it. Gestalt therapy is a means for establishing awareness of the flow and reducing or eliminating feelings or behavior that inhibit or go counter to the flow.

Gestalt techniques incorporate a lot of communication skills, awareness-focus skills (here and now, you and I), and self-responsibility emphases ("I messages") that are common to a large number of contemporary models.

There are some things that seem unique to Gestalt therapy. These include projection of self into objects, other people, or parts of experience, dialogues within self—as in "What is your stomach telling you?"—and enactments of bipolarities such as the neat and tidy versus the sloppy parts of our personality or the kind and considerate versus the selfish and insensitive parts. Through use of such techniques both personal and environmental factors that are influential but largely unnoticed are brought into focus (figure) for analysis; and a more fluid movement of factors from context (ground) to focus (figure) provides increased awareness and ability to know the flow and be an active participant, an integrated personality.

It is beyond the scope of this book to detail the various Gestalt techniques. It is helpful to recognize that clients produce complicated and often contradictory data. Careful use of the SITE skills will provide awareness of duple or multiple tendencies within a client. For example:

"You really want to lose weight *and* you really enjoy eating."

"You love your spouse *and* you feel hateful toward him/her."

"You believe in delegating responsibility, *but* you can't let the workers out of your sight because they might make mistakes."

"On the one hand . . . , *but* on the other . . . "

Many Gestalt techniques—empty chair, dialogue with parts of body or parts of dream, top dog/underdog—are mostly means of differentiating the contradictory or varying parts by giving them location, embodiment or focus. Often the importance of each is highlighted by its contrast with others. Much the same as with other tracking skills, increased awareness often allows clients to create and employ their own solutions and sometimes leaves them in the dilemma of "That's interesting, but what do I do now?"

The process of responsive therapy to this point has incorporated the initiation of therapy through management of the environment and application of the initiating skills [indirect lead, paraphrase of content, and summary of content]. Tracking skills and general process enhancers, including Gestalt techniques, accomplished the clarification phase of counseling in which the client's style, circumstances, and past efforts at coping with those circumstances were described, refined, and clarified. For those clients whose major difficulty was in gaining a clear perspective of their condition, therapy has been altered to be supportive or has ended.

For the remaining clients, who haven't the knowledge or skill to initiate and follow through with corrective procedures, the alteration phase is one of active intervention, as the therapist teaches the client one or several strategies directed at the client's specific circumstance.

The proper use of specific process enhancers will provide the most efficient therapy with the highest probability of success. Specific process enhancers, referenced by names of well-known theories or approaches to counseling, will be treated according to the following categories: cognitive, affective, behavioral. The assignment to categories is based on an analysis of the unique, problem-focused aspects of each. For a similar treatment, but with some variations of assignment, see *Methods of Self-Change* (Rudestam, 1980).

As an initial introduction, the treatment of each specific enhancement model will be brief. This is to provide an overview and "speaking acquaintance" with many models. Chapters 6, 7, and 8 will provide expansion and demonstration of one or two approaches within each of the categories—cognitive, affective, behavioral. Students are encouraged to select a model within each category and become proficient in their application of it so as to have at least one theory-pure approach in their repertoire for each category.

COGNITIVE METHODS

This section focuses on several approaches that emphasize intervention of an intellectual, thinking, or understanding nature. Proponents of each contend that both satisfying emotional and desirable behavioral change will follow the cognitive reconstruction. Whether or not the behavior and emotions are changed, these techniques do provide changes in thinking. The approaches to be considered are rational-emotive therapy, transactional analysis, bibliotherapy and cognitive homework, and brief therapy.

Rational-Emotive Therapy

This intervention approach is attributable solely to Albert Ellis, director of the Institute for Rational-Emotive Therapy.

The cornerstone is stated succinctly by Epictetus, a Roman philosopher, who said, "People are disturbed not by things, but by the views which they take of them."[1]

> Rational-Emotive Therapy (RET) is an action-oriented approach that emphasizes people's responsibility for creating their own upsetting emotions—and hence their unusual capacities to help "recondition" themselves and choose more emotionally satisfying lives.

RET posits that disturbances are chiefly caused by irrational attitudes and beliefs about oneself, others, and the surrounding world. These beliefs and values typically get reinforced during childhood, and are then perpetuated by a process of continuous negative self-reindoctrination. By learning to understand fully, then to actively dispute and uproot their unrealistic shoulds, oughts, and musts, people can develop their capacities for greatly increased self-affirmation, effectiveness, and pleasure.[1]

According to this viewpoint, behavior and emotion make up the third step in a values-mediated process. Unlike behaviorists, who would suggest that actions are a result of antecedent (stimulus-response) or consequent conditions (stimulus-response-stimulus), RET places emphasis on an intermediate, cognitive step: (a) conditions occur in the environment; (b) the person interprets and judges those conditions; and (c) the person behaves and/or emotes relative to the judgment formed. If the judgment is that conditions are ominous or deplorable, the resultant emotions would be fear or self-pity, and the actions would be flight or "resigned inactivity." If the judgment of the same conditions is that they are challenging and exciting, then markedly different feelings and actions would follow. It is this reasoning, that emotion and action grow out of interpretation, that forms the emphasis on changing the rational interpretations to produce more desirable feelings and acts.

There is a certain style to RET that is best demonstrated by quoting Ellis (1969) directly:

> Most of what we label our "emotional reactions" are caused by our conscious and unconscious evaluations, interpretations, and philosophies. Thus we feel anxious because we strongly convince ourselves that it would be terrible if we failed at something or that we couldn't stand the pain of being rejected; and we feel hostile because we vigorously believe that people who behave unfairly to us absolutely *should not* be the way they indubitably are and that it is ut-

---

[1] Advertisement for Institute for Rational-Emotive Therapy.

terly horrible that they are frustrating us. If we more sanely
convince ourselves that it is decidedly inconvenient if we
fail at something but that such a failure hardly makes us a
total loss, we change our feeling of anxiety or depression to
one of sorrow without self-deprecation; and if we change
our Jehovian hypothesis that people who behave unfairly to
us absolutely *should not* be the way they are to the more em-
pirically-based hypothesis that it would be wonderful if they
were not that way but that (a) unfortunately they are and (b)
it is clearly frustrating but not horrible that execrable behavior like theirs exists, we concomitantly change our feeling of hostility to that of unangry displeasure and a stead-
fast determination to avoid or to adequately deal with
people who behave in this unfair manner. (p. 84)

Intervention consists of verbally challenging the "irrational-
ities" spoken by clients in a strongly confrontive manner. Emotional release frequently occurs as the clients attempt to defend
or resist changing their perceptions and evaluations. Under the
strong and logical onslaught of the therapist aided by homework
and, if group therapy, by the pressure of other group members,
clients typically relinquish prior judgments in favor of those presented to them.

The focus of RET is on the here-and-now, rather than on a
historical perspective; it actively homes in on illogical reasoning
rather than patiently enduring elaboration and recounting of
symptoms; it is quick-tempoed as controlled by the therapist;
and it is usually limited to half-hour sessions plus homework.

In brief summary RET is an approach that teaches clients to
alter beliefs and judgments from those that result in disintegra-
tive emotions and self-defeating behavior to those emotions that
are useful and tolerable and those actions that are self-serving
and primarily socialized.

Transactional Analysis

Many personality theories and therapy models are explained by reference to commonly understood systems of experience. What begins as analogy frequently becomes absorbed

into the model by successive refinements of meanings. Such a process is typified by Eric Berne's development of transactional analysis (TA).

The basic unit of study is the behavior involved in a dyadic (two-person) relationship. What one person says to another and its effect in terms of a reply is analogous to a transaction; the most common meaning for transaction is in commerce, where goods or services are negotiated, paid for, and delivered.

Of course, even an ordinary business transaction can be very complex, depending on the motives, values, and skills of the participants. It may be fair and honest, or it may involve deception and dishonesty. Success in business transactions requires or at least is greatly enhanced by knowledge, by clear perception of what's being negotiated compared to a background of similar experience.

The world of commerce is sometimes called a game, another analogy based on the similarities between some business dealings and the competitive, win-lose nature of games. The winner of the game is the person shrewdest in operating within the rules. The game is more than a simple transaction, one where what is purchased is equivalent in value to the price paid for it, a condition in which there are no winners or losers, only mutual participants. In a game somebody wins and somebody loses.

Whenever a player in the game of commerce discovers a technicality or procedure that is not generally known and by which he wins great sums or wins consistently over many transactions, he is said to be operating a racket.

Berne (1961, 1964) and Harris (1967) have established and refined a personal transaction model that on the surface is very similar to the transactions, games, and rackets of commerce. The adoption of familiar language and well-known analogues makes TA a deceptively simple and enticing model. It may be this factor that has caused its widespread appeal and popularity. Underneath the deceptively simple analogy is a fairly well conceived and rather complete theory of personality development, dynamics, and pathology.

There are two divisions to Berne's model, transactional analysis and structural analysis (1961). Transactional analyses focus on an understanding and description of the dynamics of interaction between two people. The motives and style of each participant at any point in time are a result of his/her unique personality, the study of which would be structural analysis.

From a philosophy or conceptualization that is too similar to Freudian theorizing to escape comparison, each individual is postulated to be a composite of child, parent, and adult natures or styles. In a transaction, the individual will manifest one or the other of those natures depending on which is executive at that time. Here again is an analogy of a rotating chairmanship. In a very mature and well-functioning individual the executive power will reside most frequently in the adult.

Depending on degree of immaturity or pathology, the executive may be drawn somewhat forcefully into the parent or child mode (this is referred to as "Hooking the Child") or may be restrained by or imprisoned within parent or child due to boundary sclerosis.

Therapy consists of teaching the person, primarily through intellectual processes involving modeling and verbally educating the adult mode, to maintain executive function, to avoid getting hooked improperly or self-defeatingly, and yet to maintain some spontaneity of child expression and some tradition and morality of parent expression.

In brief summary TA focuses on the nature of a person as evidenced by his/her interaction with others and works to correct self-defeating styles (scripts) by altering transactions. The intended progress is from rackets and games (win-lose) to intimacy (win-win).

Bibliotherapy and Cognitive Homework

Bibliotherapy is nothing more than augmenting the client-therapist interaction by use of books and articles. It is prescriptive in nature, in that the client is directed to read specific materials at critical times in the therapeutic sequence and for specific reasons.

Biographical treatises may provide a sense of hope and lessening of isolation in the awareness that others have experienced and resolved similar problems. Humorous or entertaining reading may be prescribed as a contrast or escape from too much mentalizing over problems. Philosophical or theoretical selections are used to increase the client's understanding of foundation factors, precipitating circumstances, personal or interpersonal dynamics, or processes for remediation of his/her condition.

Cognitive homework may include, but is not limited to, reading. It may include keeping a record of thoughts, experiences, reactions, dreams. Journals and diaries would be included. Engaging in experiences or making observations, recording and analyzing reactions, or self-analysis could be involved.

Bibliotherapy and cognitive homework are typically adjunct to ongoing therapeutic contact between client and therapist. They serve to augment or provide depth or breadth to therapy sessions and to keep the client on task during intervals between sessions.

Brief Therapy

An unconventional but definitely cognitive model has grown out of contemporary hypnotherapy. Its roots include ideas from early philosophers, Freudian notions of unconscious determinants of behavior, and certain existential notions of phenomenological living and being in the world. Milton H. Erickson apparently is the primary referent for study, emulation, and focus of theorizing for a number of contemporary proponents of brief therapy. This section draws heavily on the works of Paul Watzlawick (1978) and Jay Haley (1973).

Procedurally, brief therapy employs a number of techniques geared to bypass the logically formalized means by which a client "understands" and describes his/her world and communicates more directly with that part of the mind that Freud called unconscious or preconscious; it is the "back of the mind" which hypnotists frequently address.

Rather than a "lower" part that is below consciousness, or a "back" part that is beyond consciousness, Watzlawick postulates a parallel or "by the side of" mind that is an extremely conscious but generally silent partner to the logical mind. It is silent, by and large, because few people understand how to communicate with it, how to speak its language.

Other forms of therapy are lengthy for two reasons: (a) they first teach the client a new language pertinent to the theory the therapist subscribes to, and (b) they involve long periods of waiting for spontaneous changes to occur. Brief therapy, in contrast, deals in the language of the "other" mind and stimulates spontaneous recovery or manipulates the client into self-enhancing activity.

There are two conceptual foundation stones for this model as described by Watzlawick (1978). The first comes from research on brain pathology, most notably that which involves separation of the two cerebral hemispheres. The reactions of patients with commissurotomies have stimulated many postulations of the left-brain/right-brain functions. One such postulation is that "we have two conscious minds which, ideally, are capable of harmonious, complementary integration for the purpose of grasping and mastering our inner and outer reality, but which, if and when conflict arises, may be unable to communicate with each other for lack of a common language" (Watzlawick, 1978, p. 38).

The lack of common language results from specialization in the left cerebral hemisphere (in right-handed people) for formalized language of reason, science, explanation, and interpretation, whereas the right hemisphere uses imagery, metaphor, symbolism, synthesis, and totality. The right half experiences; the left half explains.

The second foundation stone is the phenomenological assumption, the belief that each individual has a unique experience or perception of reality and that behavior is a product of the meaning attributed to the unique perception.

> Anybody seeking our help . . . suffers from his *image* of the world, from the unresolved contradiction between the way things appear to him and the way they *should be* according to his world image. He then can choose one of two alternatives: he can intervene actively in the course of events and adapt the world more or less to his image; or, where the world cannot be changed, he can adapt his image to the un-

alterable facts. The first alternative may very well be the object of advice and counselling . . . whereas the latter is more specifically the task and goal of therapy (Watzlawick, 1978, pp. 40–41).

From the two foundation stones—two conscious minds and a perceptual model of the world—the basic premise of brief therapy can be stated: *"The translation of the perceived reality, this synthesis of our experience of the world into an image, is most probably the function of the right hemisphere.* [Italics in original.] To the left half, presumably, goes the task of rationalizing this image, of separating the whole . . . into subject and object" (Watzlawick, 1978, pp. 45–46).

To the extent that the postulated premise is correct, therapeutic change will then occur as a result of three types of intervention: (a) the use of right-hemispheric language patterns, (b) blocking the left hemisphere and (c) making specific behavior prescriptions. Through the processes of communication through imagery, figurative language, illusions, and the like; confusing the logical mind with paradoxical language, illusion of alternatives, reframing, and so on; and prescribing behavioral tasks that alter the client's pattern of self-defeat, the brief therapist promotes spontaneous change. "Spontaneous change . . . obviously occurs when certain perceptions or other experiences can no longer be integrated into a person's world image . . . and thus requires at least a partial change of the image" (Watzlawick, 1978, p. 128).

Although definitely cognitive in nature, brief therapy has a unique set of presuppositions and techniques that require careful study and practice. Proponents claim that it is not necessary to incorporate hypnosis into this model, but there appears to be a decided advantage in doing so.

From therapies dealing with thoughts, images, and understanding, we turn next to therapies for emotional change. Ventilation, in the early stages of counseling, is an expression of emotion that has been pent up for some time. Its release is necessary for various kinds of intervention. If, after ventilation, emotional symptoms remain or frequently recur, active intervention of an affective nature may be called for.

Affective Methods

The emotional nature and experiences of people can be described as symptoms or outcomes of experiences. They can be seen also as an advance warning system for avoidance of damaging or life-threatening conditions. They have been postulated as a safety system for expressing or tapping off tension. Some might claim that they form a system, akin to the skeletal system or integumentary system, with a specific life-enhancing purpose. Others would possibly see them as evidence for an integration of mental and physical systems and experiences.

Affective methods give prominence to emotions, either as a system important in its own right or as a significant access to the essence of humanness. They deal with emotions as inner-directed, self-manageable, and accessible only through their owner. Most affective theorists view people as responsible, basically good, and potentially successful. Problems result from environmental circumstances that inhibit natural development or prevent normal emotional expression.

There are two divisions of affective therapy and several models in each division. The relationship therapies include nondirective counseling and humanistic methods. The manipulative therapies include body therapies and provocative therapy.

Relationship Therapies

The personal relationship between counselor and client is considered to be important by nearly all therapists. For relationship therapists it is *the* dynamic factor that allows therapeutic change.

For many clients who have little or no social support system and a history of emotional frustration and isolation, a warm, positive, and consistent relationship can provide support and validation of sufficient strength to permit them to move through the obstacles to their adjustment.

Nondirective Counseling.   Historically, therapy was seen as a process managed by the therapist and prescriptive in nature. Nondirective philosophy assumes that the experiencing individuals are in the best, most authoritative position to know what is happening. If they are experiencing dissatisfaction, unhappiness, lack of productivity, and the like, it is because they have been prevented from developing the willingness to act in their own behalf.

An environment that is not threatening and can enhance self-exploration will offer clients an opportunity to find structure in their experience, develop strong self-worth feelings, and establish procedures for resolution of their problems.

The role of the nondirective therapist is to create this kind of environment. Carl Rogers (1951, 1961) has been the foremost proponent of this approach. From his experiences and writings have evolved three major characteristics of the therapeutic environment; warmth, empathy, and unconditional positive regard. The techniques of this approach center on nonjudgmental reflection of client verbalizations and consistent, patient, long-term support of client self-exploration.

Humanistic Methods.   The nondirective approach, the existential therapy (May et al., 1958), self-actualization theory (Maslow, 1954, 1971), and several other views of personkind and therapy have come to be known as the third force, or humanistic psychology (the other two forces are psychoanalysis and behaviorism). Buhler and Bugenthal provided a brief statement of four qualities of humanistic psychology.

1. Centering of attention on the experiencing person, and thus a focus on experience as the primary phenomenon in the study of man.

2. Emphasis on such distinctively human qualities as choice, creativity, valuation, and self-realization, as opposed to thinking about human beings in mechanistic and reductionistic terms.

3. Allegiance to meaningfulness in the selection of problems for study; opposition to a primary emphasis on objectivity at the expense of significance.

4. An ultimate concern with and valuing of the dignity and worth of man and an interest in the development of the potential inherent in every person. (Sahakian, 1976, pp. 379–380)

Manipulative Therapies

Another class of therapy that evokes emotional reaction by doing something to the client is that of manipulative therapy. This is not a formal title and could be applied to some approaches outside of the affective realm. The methods that follow are nonrelational, manipulative affective techniques.

Body Therapies.   All theory has roots firmly planted in philosophy and is based logically on premises growing out of that philosophical foundation. Validation is usually a circular process and can be seen quite clearly in the body therapies.

For centuries people have debated the basic nature of humanity. Are body and mind or body and soul two separate and distinct entities (dualism)? Is there an integrated, single characteristic that incorporates all facets of life (monism)?

If the presumption is dualism, then separate treatments are in order for body ailments and mind disorders. The history of physical medicine and mental illness is strongly influenced by a dualistic philosophy. Attribution of mental illness to evil spirits, the muses, or even gifts from God made it totally separate and distinct from physical concerns (Menninger, Meyman, & Pruyser, 1963). To follow up on the notion of circular validation, if treatments designed to alter the body are successful, then direct intervention into the troubled system is the treatment of choice and requires no concern for separate systems.

If the presumption is monism, then any type of therapeutic intervention will affect the entire system. It would be possible to effect positive emotional state by establishing a healthy physical condition; good mental status would similarly enhance physical functioning. Conversely, mental stresses would be seen as causal factors in physical disease, and physical deterioration or disease would produce negative mental or emotional conditions. Psychosomatic medicine and the holistic health movement are based on the monistic tradition. Circular validation of the monistic premise would occur when treatment modalities based on it produced total system changes, or when psychotherapy produced physical improvement and medical treatment removed emotional symptoms.

The body therapies are based largely on the notion that body segments or body systems, mostly the integumentary and musculature systems, are repositories of the effects of emotional conditions; i.e., people store the residue of tension in their muscles. This being the case, it is then possible to act directly on those systems to loosen up the tensions and permit the body to return to normal functioning.

One of the early body therapists, Wilhelm Reich (1927), believed that there are seven regions of the body, which he called rings of armoring, that must be progressively broken to free the person from residual tensions. Lowen and his bioenergetics (1975) and Rolf with her rolfing (1975) are contemporary practitioners who have established systems of direct body manipulation by the therapist to aid in the removal of mental or emotional maladies.

Provocative Therapy.   Based similarly on the notion that emotions get stored up or blocked in people who have emotional illness is a system for eliciting expression of those emotions. Farrelly and Brandsma (1974) have pioneered what they call provocative therapy. This approach can be summarized as an attempt to cause the client to marshal his emotional resources in defense of himself against the barrage of badgering, belittling, and insulting verbalizations of the therapist. This is seen by many therapists as a highly specific, narrow-band technique, to be used selectively on a few clients. Farrelly and Brandsma profess success in a number of conditions and for a variety of clients.

From a concentration on methods that aim directly at emotional well-being we turn to a category of models that, by and large, ignores emotion. The belief is that if the problematic behavior or symptom is removed, there is no need to feel anything but okay.

This section involves behavioral methods that address symptom removal. They are behavior modification, contingency management, structural family therapy, and reciprocal inhibition. The following section will deal with behavioral techniques for acquisition of social skills.

BEHAVIORAL: SYMPTOM CONTROL METHODS

On the assumption that there is no deep-seated personality disturbance that causes problematic or self-defeating actions, the behaviorist proceeds to alter directly the symptoms of distress. Quite simply, the symptom is the disorder. The following are four models for symptom removal, alteration, or control.

Behavior Modification

This approach is simply an application of operant techniques devised by B. F. Skinner and tested thoroughly on rats and other subhuman species. Control of behavior happens as a result of environmental dynamics that become learned as signals and outcomes related to specific behavior. When a response is made by a person in a circumstance that has perceptible characteristics, and a change in condition occurs that increases the probability of that same (or very similar) behavior occurring in the same (or very similar) circumstance, behavior has been modified.

Repetition of a behavior that results in absolutely no change of condition generally results in cessation of that behavior. This is the extinction process.

Application of behavior modification is concerned with either the process of establishing an absent but desirable response, removing a present and undesirable response, or both.

The procedure follows, in some form, these basic steps:

1. Identify the target behavior.
2. Measure or systematically count occurrences of that behavior.
3. Determine what consequences are currently supporting the continuation of an undesirable behavior or what outcomes, if added following a desirable behavior, will increase its probability of recurrence.
4. Cause the person to exhibit (a) undesirable behavior in the absence of its reinforcer, hence extinguishing it, or (b) desirable behavior with the consequence of an outcome that increases its tendency to recur.

5. Measure target behavior again to see if the expected changes have occurred.

Behavior modification techniques are especially applicable to environmentally cued habits; some examples are overeating, smoking, poor concentration, and language difficulties.

Contingency Management

The theoretical bases for contingency management and behavior modification are identical. The primary distinction, which is not uniformly made by all practitioners, is that behavior modification is applied to a single client in a therapeutic setting, whereas contingency management is creating and maintaining a system for groups of people or for individuals in a group setting.

Precision teaching, Premack principle, token economy, programmed learning, computer-assisted instruction and behavior contracting are all applications of contingency management. The basic procedures include the following:

1. Defining the desired terminal behavior.
2. Establishing reinforcers, usually more than one so as to account for differences in individual preference, which are to be given contiguously or nearly so to acceptable approximations of the desired behavior.
3. A system for continuous monitoring and application of the reinforcers.

Although both contingency management and behavior modification appear to involve artificial manipulation of clients through application of extrinsic rewards, a rather convincing case can be made for its near parallel to "Mother Nature's" methods and her intrinsic outcomes.

Structural Family Therapy

During the 1950s several therapists began the process of shifting focus from the individual as client to dealing with identifiable systems or social contexts. The family became identified as a system that functions or malfunctions with symptomatic import on its members (Haley, 1971). The initial movement was simply a change of definition of client from individual to family and involved relatively little change in theoretical or procedural approach; i.e., each therapist employed his/her preferred techniques within the appropriate theoretical context. One method that has evolved as uniquely a family or family system approach is structural family therapy.

Perhaps the foremost proponent of this approach is Salvador Minuchin (1974). He defines structural family therapy as "a body of theory and techniques that approaches the individual in his social context. Therapy based on this framework is directed toward changing the organization of the family" (p. 2).

In Minuchin's description of three "axioms" of his approach, there is a distinct flavor of reciprocal determinism a la Bandura (1978); however, descriptions of therapeutic intervention appear to be directed at changing the social-environmental field in order to alter the balance of forces acting on the individual, thus causing him/her to behave differently. This is similar in some respects to Lewinian Field Theory (Cartwright, 1951).

The three "axioms" are as follows:

> 1. . . . an individual's psychic life is not entirely an internal process. The individual influences his context and is influenced by it in constantly recurring sequences of interaction. The individual who lives within a family is a member of a social system to which he must adapt. His actions are governed by the characteristics of the system, and these characteristics include the effects of his own past actions. The individual responds to stresses in other parts of the system, to which he adapts; and he may contribute significantly to stressing other members of the system. The individual can be approached as a subsystem, or part, of the system, but the whole must be taken into account.
>
> 2. . . . changes in a family structure contribute to changes in the behavior and the inner psychic processes of the members of that system.
>
> 3. . . . when a therapist works with a patient or a pa-

tient family, his behavior becomes part of the context. Therapist and family join to form a new, therapeutic system, and that system then governs the behavior of its members. (Minuchin, 1974, p. 9)

A picture is presented of a family system, a sort of homeostatic entity wherein change in one part causes changes in other parts. The system seems to transcend its members. A healthy system is one that is flexible enough to adjust to member variations. "Responding to . . . demands from both within and without requires a constant transformation of the position of family members in relation to one another, so they can grow while the family system maintains continuity" (Minuchin, 1974, p. 60). Pathology occurs when the ability to be flexible is absent, and instead the family reacts to stress by increasing the rigidity of its transactional patterns.

The task of the therapist is to enter the system, diagnose the functionally rigid portions, institute appropriate adjustments, and then exit the system, leaving it to function autonomously. This is somewhat analogous to a mechanic who trouble-shoots out the malfunction, adjusts the critical parts, and then leaves it alone until some future breakdown. Much as with the automobile, the critical component in the malfunction is not always the one that shows the symptom.

"Change is seen as occurring through the process of the therapist's affiliation with the family and his restructuring of the family in a carefully planned way, so as to transform dysfunctional transactional patterns" (Minuchin, 1974, p. 91). Because therapeutic change in an individual occurs through intervention in the system, the individual's function is dependent on the system, this model fits quite nicely into an environmentally determined, stimulus-control framework.

Reciprocal Inhibition

Of several applications of Pavlov's work, later dubbed classical conditioning, the most refined and currently used system is that of Wolpe (1973). The basic notion is that emotional response is the result of the contiguous linking of a strongly obvious environmental condition and viscerogenic or autonomic reactions. These emotional learnings are possibly useful or, at worst, harmless in their normal manifestations; however, when abnormal, as in phobias or high anxiety states, they are very self-defeating.

The opposite of a high-arousal, high emotional state is deep relaxation. Wolpe postulated that if the inappropriate emotional response were a result of improper learning, then a more useful response could be conditioned into the person, which would compete with or inhibit the maladaptive one; hence, reciprocal (opposite to maladaptive) inhibition (prevention of responding).

Procedurally, the client is first instructed in methods of deep relaxation. He/she is then put through a series of vicarious experiences that gradually, so as not to upset the relaxed state, approximate the high anxiety or phobic situation. Once the client can experience the signals for emotional upset and at the same time respond with relaxation, his/her newly learned response set overpowers or inhibits the earlier, problematic response.

Closely aligned with symptom-control methods, in that they produce socially acceptable behavior as replacement for ineffective or antisocial behavior, are the models in the following section. They are labeled vicarious reinforcement, modeling, reality therapy, and neuro-linguistic programming.

BEHAVIORAL: SOCIAL SKILLS METHODS

This section includes the term *behavioral* because the methods are directed toward producing changes in observable behavior. It draws heavily on the works of Bandura (1969, 1974, 1978), Bandura and Walters (1963), Glasser (1965), and Bandler and Grinder (1975, 1976, 1979), none of whom are theoretically aligned with behaviorists of the operant conditioning variety.

Both Bandura and Glasser see the individual as an active, potentially responsible participant in his/her cognitively mediated responses. Both accept the importance of environmental conditions as influences in behavior. Bandler and Grinder place the problem as improper links between deep structure (unverbalized determinants) and language as a control model.

Vicarious Reinforcement

One means for altering the behavior of a client is to show him/her examples—pictures, movies, videotapes, live models—of people engaging in desirable behavior and receiving positive returns for their behavior. Much of modern movie and television fare relies on the viewer to identify with the person of focus (hero, victim, antihero) and vicariously share his/her plight and outcome. Advertisements are replete with suggestions, both overt and covert, that paying for and using a product will produce for the consumer the same results, or very similar ones, that they presumably did for the advertisement model.

As therapists, it is possible to use imaginary or representational people as tools to influence change on the part of clients.

Modeling

Related to and a part of vicarious reinforcement is modeling. It is treated separately to focus on the effectiveness of using a model to demonstrate alternative behavior strategies to clients without drawing attention to an obvious reinforcement. The therapist who deals calmly with the client's crisis is likewise modeling an alternative response. Identification with or problems in identifying with exemplary models in the client's social environment provides input for problem analysis and/or resolution strategies.

Reality Therapy

This approach, popularized by William Glasser (1965), might well be called a cognitively mediated behavior modification approach. Although the outcomes of a person's behavior occur in a social context and operate somewhat predictively, the client needs to learn that proper management of reality, responsibility, and right-and-wrong will produce more consistently desirable outcomes.

That the focus is on change of behavior is demonstrated in the foreword of Glasser's book (1965): "human beings get into emotional binds, not because their standards are too high, but because their performance has been, and is, too low" (p. xiii).

In its original form reality therapy was applied to incarcerated juveniles. The procedure, tersely stated, was to produce a simplified environment where the relationship between behavior and outcome could be readily apparent and constant. The inmate soon gained the insight that the outcome for herself was under her control; she found that she was responsible.

In clinical application, effort is made to help clients see the relationship between their behavior and its self-defeating outcome, and then to learn alternative actions. Some attempt to modify the environment may occur, but the major impetus is toward creating in the client an awareness of self-responsibility. Part of this process is for the therapist to avoid taking any responsibility for the condition and outcome and to refuse to acknowledge any outside responsibility.

Neuro-Linguistic Programming (NLP)

This particular model is difficult to place neatly in the categories. It contains some reference to cognitive function (language as a meta-model); there is a Gestalt or integrational flavor (seeing, hearing, feeling as routes to experience); and there is a classical conditioning emphasis (stimulus substitution and signal learning). Because the favored intervention seems to be a reconditioning or reprogramming, the model is placed in the behavioral section. Because the reprogramming is done with unverbalized or precognitive aspects of the personality and is therefore similar in some respect to vicarious conditioning, it is placed in the section with Bandura and Glasser.

Problems of adjustment or incidents of self-defeating behavior occur as a result of the way people learn to explain their reality. In essence, they build a language theory or model of reality and then work from the model rather than from the reality on which it is based.

In the process of model building most people adopt a preference for seeing (visualizing), hearing, or feeling as a means of access to the world. Their chosen modality tends to dominate the "program" on which they operate.

The goal of the NLP therapist is to increase options, hence

variability, for the clients so that they can avoid self-defeat. Access to the client's process style is achieved by discovering the preferred mode of experiencing. Through appeals to that mode, or through a variety of techniques to bypass it, a new program is established that includes the old choices as well as a number of alternate ones.

The solution of problems is not in the identification of preferred experiential mode, nor is it in the integration of the three modes. The modes simply provide access to the deeper structure where classical conditioning processes called anchoring, bridging, and changing history are performed.

Anchoring is the process of associating a condition or attitude with a therapist-controlled stimulus (stimulus substitution), such as a touch on one shoulder, a word, or an eye fixation. Subsequently, the new stimulus can be used to elicit the condition or attitude. Usually an alternate program (behavior, belief, attitude) is vicariously established and anchored to a similar stimulus; e.g., a touch on the other shoulder.

Bridging occurs as a result of stimulating both anchors simultaneously and/or by ritualistically combining vicarious ways of coping (visualizations or auditory or kinesthetic hallucinations). The result is an "integrated" program that allows either previous choice or selective modifications or combinations.

Changing history is a process of anchoring the memory of some aspect of personal history (which is often not factual) and bridging that anchored memory to a more acceptable, created memory. Reality is not changed, but the model (which determines behavior and satisfaction) is altered in such a way as to provide more choice and more control to the client.

A key concept in NLP is process. The content of verbalizations is not significant except as a clue to referential modes, and since eye motions or other cues are available to identify process, it is possible to produce therapeutic change without knowing a verbal description of the problem.

Although Bandler and Grinder claim that it is not necessary to know hypnosis in order to do NLP therapy, their background and many of the philosophical underpinnings of the model suggest that such knowledge would be very advantageous to anyone adopting this approach.

One additional characteristic of NLP therapy is variability in modifications of therapy. If something does not work, the problem is assigned to the therapy and not to the client. "If what you are doing is not working, change it. Do something else" (Bandler & Grinder, 1979, p. 73).

As a brief comparative digression, it appears that a major contrast between NLP and social learning is that the NLP therapist behaves like the client (mirrors) in order to understand and expand options from within. The social learning therapist presents examples (models) for the client to approximate as a means of increasing options from without. It may be that mirroring and modeling are two sides of the same coin.

Selection of Method

The previous descriptions of methods comprise a very brief overview. Quite obviously, people choosing to use any of them should become thoroughly educated in their underlying philosophies, techniques, and appropriate applications. It is not helpful, and probably damaging, to employ techniques indiscriminately and without sound preparation.

Assuming proper preparation in several treatment methods and sufficient knowledge of others to afford sensible referral, the next problem is determining which method to employ or to which therapist a referral should be made.

The early phases of therapy, managed by use of the SITE skills, enable the therapist to reconstruct major elements of the client's phenomenological space and to monitor ways in which the client has attempted to manage his/her world. The client styles related to understanding, feeling okay, and outcome control as described in the section dealing with cognitive, affective, and behavioral modes of preference provide a framework for describing the ways the client has tried unsuccessfully to cope with problems.

A problem is basically nothing more than a condition that needs to be changed, possessed by a person who does not know how to change it. This lack of knowledge may be categorized as the presence of self-defeating behavior or attitudes, lack of awareness or understanding, and lack of requisite skills.

The appropriate therapeutic method to be applied from the narrow-band, specific-enhancing-skill category is that one (or those) that most efficiently removes the behavioral or attitudinal block or that provides the necessary awareness or skill. Once again, it is important to point out that the therapy of choice often may counter the client's preferred style because of his/her overreliance on that preferred style.

Figure 5-11 illustrates the dynamics of moving through the funnel to identify the critical factors, styles, and problems and then "dumping" them into the appropriate methodological receptacle. Please note that the receptacles are discrete, mutually exclusive, theory-pure methods. It is common for different problems within the same client system to be treated by different but selectively appropriate methods within the same time frame. As Cormier and Cormier (1979) point out, "A variety of strategies is necessary in order to treat the complexity and range of problems presented by a single client. It is just not that common to encounter a client with only one very straightforward concern (such as fear of flying in airplanes) that can be treated successfully with only one strategy (such as systematic desensitization)" (p. 255).

The next three chapters will illustrate approaches in each of the three categories—cognitive, affective, behavioral.

Summary

Therapy proceeds in an orderly manner through initiation, tracking, and general enhancing to arrive at an awareness of specific problems and client styles. At this point the selection of appropriate methods or process enhancers specific to the client's needs and style can be made.

Internal congruence, or a balancing of the cognitive, affective, and behavioral components of personality, is a common goal of therapy. Unresolved problems are accompanied by an imbalance in these components or a state of internal incongruence.

Clients vary in their reliance on or preference for working with one of the personality components, sometimes to the exclu-

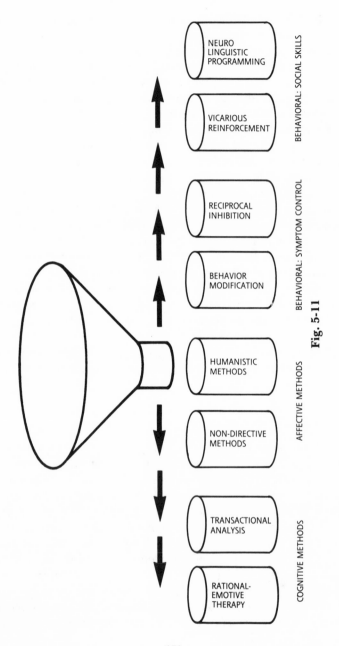

BEHAVIORAL: SOCIAL SKILLS

NEURO LINGUISTIC PROGRAMMING

VICARIOUS REINFORCEMENT

BEHAVIORAL: SYMPTOM CONTROL

RECIPROCAL INHIBITION

BEHAVIOR MODIFICATION

AFFECTIVE METHODS

HUMANISTIC METHODS

NON-DIRECTIVE METHODS

COGNITIVE METHODS

TRANSACTIONAL ANALYSIS

RATIONAL-EMOTIVE THERAPY

Fig. 5-11

sion of the other two. People can be seen to treat understanding as the means to all problem resolution; others validate success by how they feel; and still others operate very much as though they are controlled by external conditions and factors. Obviously, not all people fit neatly into one of the three categories. The three categories can be further subdivided. Psychodynamics is the term that refers to the interaction among subparts of the personality.

Probably growing out of the therapists' preferred modes or styles or from the tendency for certain types of clients to congregate at hospitals, clinics, schools, jails, or other therapeutic settings, the various counseling or therapy methods reflect stylistic patterns that tend to fit certain clients or conditions but do not work with others.

Methods can be grouped according to their stylistic techniques and underlying philosophies. One such grouping consists of four categories: (a) cognitive methods, (b) affective methods, (c) behavioral (symptom-control) methods, and (d) behavioral (social-skills) methods.

Rather than narrowly specializing in one method or even in one category, students of therapy are advised to know thoroughly at least one method from each of the categories and to be acquainted with many others. They are also advised to employ their chosen methods in a theory-pure manner sensitively matched to the client problem and style for which it is the most appropriate method.

Chapter 6

A COGNITIVE MODEL

Each person has a unique view of the world and his/her place among the many forces within that world view. Language is a tool that permits labeling and describing what is going on. Of course, if people are not aware of what is happening around them, there is no need for communicating; awareness or perception is the first stage of cognition (thinking). The urge to figure out *what* is going on and *why* it is the way it is, can lead people into (a) a comfortable state of understanding, (b) the counterfeit comfort of believing in a false conception, or (c) the discomfort of owning an explanation that they know is not entirely accurate or not quite adequate.

This dilemma of knowledge and false knowledge is depicted in this little homily of unknown origin:

> He who knows not and knows not he knows not,
> He is a fool—shun him;
> He who knows not and knows he knows not,
> He is simple—teach him;
> He who knows and knows not he knows,

He is asleep—wake him,
He who knows and knows he knows,
He is wise—follow him.

Bandler and Grinder (1975) talk of language as a *meta model*, which is a model of a model. Since models are simplifications of the real thing, language would be a simplification of a simplification. The world experience is very complex, with far more happening at one time than people are able to manage. Through the dynamics of perception they focus on one or two things intently, are aware of several other things peripherally, and shut out other, presumably less important sensations or happenings. Perception is the first model or the first simplification.

In order to communicate what is perceived, the features of perception must be labeled with words. There is a tendency to label (but with individualized interpretation) the most prominent features in focus and only some of the peripheral factors. Language, then, becomes a model or simplification of perception.

Verbal descriptions of experience are one kind of memory, and it is useful to people in directing future behavior. Much like a road map, the remembered language provides guidance for actions. If the verbal map is inaccurate in any way, behavior will be ineffective or self-defeating.

As people are observed on the continuum from retarded or unintelligent to extremely bright, their language models do not necessarily increase in accuracy. The models of more highly intelligent people tend, however, to be more complex, more differentiated, and much more elaborate than those from lesser intellects. Because they are fancier and include correct-sounding words and phrases, the more elaborate models are generally more believable, even though no more correct than others.

Given the counselor's persistent and successful initiation of therapy and accurate tracking through the use of the SITE skills, what is to be done if the client's basic representation of reality is illogical, confused, and self-defeating? What if the style is very cognitive, with the model well exercised and defended against argument? The answers lie in understanding the basic assumptions of cognitive intervention, the type of clients and circumstances responsive to cognitive intervention, and the dynamics of applying the techniques.

The understanding of ineffective language models requires working backward from the client's statements to the underlying messages. From messages the therapist can deduce the problematic or confusing logic that is supporting improper models, which in turn give rise to self-defeating actions. It is imperative that the counselor be able to hear messages in order to use cognitive interventions.

A cognitive model that can be readily applied, once the illogical messages are heard, is rational-emotive therapy (Ellis, 1973). It is not necessary to limit oneself to Ellis's style or to his value system in order to apply the principles of RET. The remainder of this chapter will be devoted to RET and includes numerous stylistic variations.

From a simple analysis of cognitive-mediated activity it can be said that there are three stages. The first is the stimulus circumstances or *activating events*. These are conditions that have some importance to an individual and necessitate some response.

The second stage happens within the individual. It is the processing of those activating events within the context of the person's *belief system*. This belief system is incorporated from all the language model representations from past experience. It is here that cognitive confusion or cognitive accuracy resides.

After activating events are interpreted through the belief system, the individual takes some action. This action is the *consequence*, not of the activating event but of the interpretation by the individual. Every action makes sense when viewed in the phenomenal perspective of the actor. Every action is the person's best choice as determined by his/her belief system.

Activating events (A) provide data for the *belief system* (B) to use in making choices from among alternative actions, the chosen one being the *consequence* (C) that is evident in the behavior and experience of the person. That different consequences happen from the same activating experiences can be seen in this example:

Activating event—Student is asked by professor to come in and talk following the return of an exam that the student failed.

Belief system 1—The teacher is angry and disappointed, or he/she would not have called me in.

Consequence 1—Defensiveness, distance, excuse-making, tension, unenjoyable encounter.

Belief system 2—The teacher likes me and cares enough to inquire into circumstances regarding my poor performance.

Consequence 2—Gratitude, openness, free communication, satisfying interaction.

Because the belief system is accessed through language, it is common to refer to the sentences people tell themselves when interpreting the activating events. If the therapist can accurately verbalize those "internal sentences," he/she can then take steps to alter them. Ellis (1973) uses the term *dispute* in reference to working on illogical ideas that are a part of the belief system. He has a list of frequently subscribed, inane beliefs that are particularly common.

1. The idea that it is a dire necessity for an adult human to be loved or approved by virtually every significant other person in his/her life.
2. The idea that one should be thoroughly competent, adequate, and achieving in all possible respects to consider oneself worthwhile.
3. The idea that certain people are bad, wicked, or villainous and that they should be severely blamed and punished for their villainy.
4. The idea that it is awful and catastrophic when things are not the way one would like them to be.
5. The idea that human unhappiness is externally caused and that people have little or no ability to control their terrors and disturbances.
6. The idea that it is easier to avoid than to face life's difficulties and self-responsibilities.
7. The idea that one's past history is an all-important determiner of one's present behavior and that, because

> something once strongly affected one's life, it should
> definitely continue to do so. (p. 37)

Although Ellis prefers and recommends an active confrontation of the illogical beliefs and a belittling of the person who would continue their use, it is possible to evoke change by softer confrontation, increase of perceptual field, reframing (helping client see/say things from a different perspective), tutoring, role play, and rehearsal.

The assumptions included in the above discussion are the following:

1. People make choices before taking action.
2. Choices are limited by options available from the belief system.
3. Changes in action require changes in the belief system.
4. It is imperative for the therapist to hear messages accurately in order to initiate proper changes in the belief system of the client.

APPROPRIATE CLIENTELE

The first and foremost criterion for application of cognitive techniques is that clients be intelligent enough and have a well-developed language model. Children under eight to ten years of age and people with comparable intellectual development, even though older, are not promising candidates for cognitive techniques. Reasoning with a child is extremely inefficient.

Another criterion, although obvious, bears formal statement. Cognitive approaches are best applied to people who have cognitive problems; e.g., illogical belief systems, value binds, confusion, a history of foolish or stupid decisions. Clients whose major disturbance lies in emotional or habitual self-defeating actions are better treated by affective or behavioral interventions.

One type of client for whom cognitive approaches are particularly useful is the person whose behavior is not congruent with his/her value system and who goes to great length to rationalize away the discrepancy.

DYNAMICS

The process of cognitive intervention requires the following:

1. Tracking accurately to ascertain *activating events.*
2. Hearing of messages to determine "internal sentences" and segments of belief system.
3. Description of situation so as to identify repetitions or patterns of illogically mediated *consequences* and specific cognitive style of client.
4. Selective use of interventions that serve to challenge or dispute the illogical beliefs. These will be selected primarily in response to the client's style.
   (a) Strong confrontation and belittling—"That's incredibly stupid."
   (b) Soft confrontation—"Could it be be that . . ?"
   (c) Increasing perceptual field—"What are other possible explanations?"
   (d) Reframing—"Describe the same circumstance in positive words."
   (e) Tutoring—"Say after me, 'I really *don't* have to . . .'"
   (f) Role play—"Go through that again with the following changes . . ."
   (g) Rehearsal—"Each morning before leaving home, say . . ."

Although the choice of techniques will vary from client to client and occasion to occasion, some notion of their application can be achieved from the next section.

EXAMPLES OF APPLICATION

Sometimes clients will repeatedly use the same illogical form. More common, however, is the tendency to include many different forms in no particular pattern. The following examples represent a cross section of a variety of client statements and possible counselor responses. The labels for groups of responses are intended for reference only and are not diagnostic labels. The labels and other systems such as Ellis's list on page 177 are attempts to catalog experiences. The therapist will make many mistakes by trying to fit actual client statements into the catalog. Although it may be interesting to compare clients with textbook lists, it is not conducive to good therapy. The importance is to hear what the messages are, identify what is not logical within the context of the client's space, and apply appropriate interventions. The challenge is to "read" the client, not the catalog.

Delusion

> *Client A:*   He was telling her awful things about me that just are not true. He is trying to sway her away from me so that she will go with him after the divorce.
>
> Illogical position: The only explanation is . . . , or since the explanation makes sense, it is correct.
>
> *Therapist Response (TR):* What is another possible explanation for his action?
>
> *Client B:*   I can never forgive myself. I'm no good. How could any worthwhile person do such a rotten thing?
>
> Illogical position: Only rotten people do rotten things.
>
> *TR:*   I've done a bad thing; therefore I'm a bad person. Since everybody does bad things on occasion, every person is bad—or could it be that good people sometimes do bad things? If other people who behave in a stupid manner can be forgiven, so can you. Stupidity is not terminal.

"Poor Me" or Self-Pity

> *Client A:*   I worked so hard and invested months of time and effort into getting that job, and he walks right in and lands it in one meeting. It's not fair.
>
> Illogical position: There is equity in life, and

those who expend the effort *should* get the result.

TR: Where is it written that life is fair? You have at least two options: one, you can sit around despairing and reveling in self-pity; or two, you can get on with life by working on the next opportunity. Of course, it's up to you, but nursing that beautiful case of "poor me" seems really dumb!

Client B: Why should I try? I'm awkward, ugly, broke, and not very bright. What's the use? I can't be anything more than a maid.

Illogical position A: Circumstances or external characteristics determine happiness.

Illogical position B: Exerting any effort in my own behalf would really be foolish.

Illogical position C: People who are as much of a waste as I am deserve pity and charity.

TR-A: There's just no hope for me. I can't be successful at things that would make me happy, and I *refuse* to be happy doing what I can.

TR-B: Anybody investing any effort into such a lost cause as I am would be really foolish. I'm not so foolish as to invest in my own future.

TR-C: I'm trying really hard to feel bad about you and your terrible plight, but you're doing such a good job of pitying yourself that I can't quite bring myself to give you more. The same amount of effort on a worthwhile cause could produce impressive results.

Blaming

Client: If it hadn't been for his constant interruption, I could have done it perfectly. Creeps like him should be put in the stocks.

Illogical position: It's terrible that other people do not act the way I want them to.

TR: It's his fault you did poorly. There was no way

you could have done differently. It was totally out of your control. He really victimized you, so you can be justifiably angry.

Egocentricity

Client: I don't want to do that. I don't like it. Why should I have to do such a thing?

Illogical position: *My* preference should determine my activity. People shouldn't have to do anything they don't want to.

TR: Liking or disliking it is your choice. Your doing it or getting fired is your boss's choice. You don't have to like it, but you do have to do it if you want to keep your job.

Historical Set

Client A: Why would he do such a thing?

Illogical position: Knowing why will somehow make things okay.

TR: Time spent in figuring out why is time wasted in finding a solution.

Client B: What caused it to happen?

Illogical position: Knowing what caused it will make a difference.

TR: It really makes little difference. What are we going to do about it?

Moral Drive

Client: I should do a better job. A person like me ought to be more competent. I just have to get it together.

Illogical position: I am not in a position to judge myself. I must please father, mother, or whoever makes the *shoulds* and *oughts* and *musts*.

TR: (The therapist recognizes the unspoken *but*) I should *but* I don't want to; I ought to *but* I won't.

Somehow there's a part of me that's not really convinced. In reality, I have a choice, and apparently I'm choosing not to do it well.

Urgency

Client: I just have to [must] pass that class so I can keep my scholarship.

Illogical position: It will be terrible, catastrophic if I don't perform well.

TR: What's the best outcome you could hope for? What's the worst that could possibly happen? What would you do if the worst occurred? What's most likely to happen?

You've said that you can handle the worst, if necessary, and that the probable is much better, so the energy you're expending on worry over the not-too-terrible could be put to much better use in assuring the probable or better.

Excuses

Client: I would really like to go to a club meeting in the city, but my husband won't take me, and I don't have a driver's license, so I won't be able to go.

Illogical position: Somebody or something else controls me, or if the easy solutions don't work, the harder ones won't either.

TR: He controls my life, and if he doesn't want to take me, then I'm utterly helpless to take care of myself. There's just no way I can manage on my own. I'm totally at his mercy.

Emotional Sellout

Client A: He makes me so mad!

Illogical position: I am not in control of my emotions.

TR: You choose to be angry. You are choosing to let him get to you.

> *Client B:*   It is so depressing.
>
> Illogical position: I am not in control of my emotions.
>
> *TR:*   I'm choosing to feel depressed rather than attempt to change things or to accept them as they are.

"Catch 22"

> *Client:*   I really should go home for the holidays. My parents are looking forward to having me there. The gang is going to vacation in Mexico, and it was sort of my idea. I don't think I can let them down. What am I going to do?
>
> Illogical position: My job is to please others. Obviously, this is a losing proposition in such a double-approach conflict.
>
> *TR-A:*   I have three choices. I can go home, please my parents, and offend my friends. I can go to Mexico, please my friends, and offend my folks. I can go someplace else and offend both my parents and friends. Since somebody will be offended anyway, I might as well do what I want to do—that way I can be sure that at least one person is pleased.
>
> *TR-B:*   My parents and friends are all dependent on me to have a good time. They will surely be reduced to tears if I fail them. They'll hold it against me forever.

Internal Duplicity

There are a number of binds that people create for themselves by adopting two opposing illogical positions and then carrying on an endless debate between the two parts of their cognitive structure. The following are some examples:

1. Attractive young woman, daughter of minister, and lady of the street.

2. Businessperson, ruthlessly aggressive in taking advantage of profitable opportunities (greedy) and benefactor of a local charity.
3. Middle-aged man, recent convert to a fundamentalist church with strong antismoking set and recent heir to a large tobacco farm.
4. Accident victim, former successful athlete, now confined to a wheelchair.

Although these circumstances do not require cognitive duplicity, they often are accompanied by it. The strategy is usually to separate out the competing positions and deal with each separately. For example, consider a woman in her early twenties, the victim of a congenital defect that caused a tremendously distorted physique and generally unattractive appearance. Her circular argument was something like "I want to date and get married and live a normal life, but nobody will accept such an ugly person; but I'm normal in most respects; but nobody will give me a chance, so why try; but if I do not try, I'll never succeed; but if I try, I'll get rejected. The possibility of succeeding won't let me rest. The probability of failing won't let me try."

Illogical positions: I am basically normal; normal people succeed easily. I am basically abnormal; abnormal people surely fail.

TR: "Your contents are intact, okay, attractive, normal, or even above average. Your package is crumpled. Nobody will choose a crumpled package. Almost anybody would like the contents.

"Let's talk from the normal-contents side for awhile. People who are normal succeed pretty easily. Your intellectual ability is normal so you breeze through school—no? But normal people have it easy. Either you're not normal intellectually, or normal people don't always have it easy. It's possible that your normal contents would not be easily successful even if you had a normal package.

"Let's talk about your package—totally repugnant. Nobody can stand to be around you—no? Some people tolerate you, even like you? Then either you're not as bad as you say, or abnormal people sometimes succeed.

"So it appears that you are 'no-ing' yourself, that is, not giving yourself or others a chance because you can't stand rejection like a normal person. You're so intent on failing that you are causing yourself to fail—self-fulfilling prophecy. I suppose it's one thing to have somebody reject you, but it's pretty stupid to do it to yourself. Of course, if you want to stay on that merry-go-round, you can. Frankly, I'm not too interested in listening more to you rejecting yourself and then crying because you feel rejected."

From the examples a certain style can be recognized. It is mildly sarcastic, almost cutting at times. Unless combined with good eye contact, supportive nonverbals, and a good relationship from good use of SITE skills, it might well push clients away rather than ahead. The use of overstatement in a paraphrase modality tends to be confrontive without being combative. It is one of many ways for using cognitive interventions.

There are, of course, limitations and cautions to using cognitive techniques. One certainly is the need to refine a style that is responsive to client conditions and yet productive. Other concerns are expressed in the next section.

LIMITATIONS AND CAUTIONS

The biggest caution is to be sure the problem is really in the cognitive realm. Because therapists are highly educated, there is a great tendency to slide into a cognitive approach and to fall into some of the same logic traps of clients; e.g., analyzing, asking why, and so on. The cognitive approaches are by far the easiest to use and the easiest to misuse of all the various kinds of techniques. The biggest category of misuse is applying them to noncognitive problems.

When clients say things like "It doesn't make sense to me" or "If only I could figure it out," the probability is that they are trying to use a cognitive approach to an affective or behavioral problem. The reason they can't figure it out is that it doesn't follow the rules and patterns of logic. The counselor who slips into the trap of trying, with the client, to figure out "what really is" and how it's affecting the client, will most likely join the client, lost in space (phenomenal space).

All of the cautions about listening for messages and not getting caught up in elaborate descriptions or self-diagnosis that were given earlier in the book are very important here.

As the therapist begins to teach clients to refute their illogical positions, he/she must constantly monitor the process. The most beautiful lesson is a waste if it doesn't fit within the client's phenomenal picture.

One other caution of importance is to remember that the therapist's task is to break clients out of an illogical position, not to see that clients accept the therapist's values or logic. Whichever of several acceptable patterns is acceptable to clients and effective in getting them out of the confines of their illogical box is the one to go with. One person's logic may violate another person's value structure in disruptive ways.

By way of limitations, the most important thing to remember is that cognitive methods are less effective in resolving affective and behavioral problems than are techniques that operate on the rules particular to each of those areas.

SUMMARY

Cognitive methods are based on principles that are tied very closely to verbal learning. What people process intellectually is done through words. Words are a representation of experiences; as such, their meaning is subject to personalization and distortion. The conclusions from experience form value statements or belief systems that are used for future decisions. If the belief system is inaccurate or illogical, behavior will be self-defeating, and emotions will be discomforting.

Activating events occur in the environment; people interpret these events by use of their belief system and then behave consequentially to their interpretation. All action, therefore, results from choice. Changes in behavioral patterns require alterations in the belief system so that more effective choices can be made.

Clients must be sufficiently intelligent and have difficulties of a cognitive nature in order to benefit from cognitive interventions.

The dynamics of cognitive intervention require effective use of SITE skills to identify *activating events, consequences,* the intervening "internal sentences," and the selective use of interventions which result in changes in illogical ideas within the *belief system.*

Applications will probably be stylized by the therapist. These applications will be made to frequently occurring patterns of client response, including delusion, "poor me" or self-pity, blaming, egocentricity, historical set, moral drive, urgency, excess, emotional sellout, "catch 22," and internal duplicity.

The most prominent cautions regarding cognitive models relate to making sure that a cognitive problem is being addressed and to avoid counselor preference for using the easy but frequently misused approaches.

The major limitation of cognitive approaches is that they are not as effective as more direct approaches to affective and behavioral problems and hence should be relinquished in favor of the more appropriate methods in noncognitive problem areas.

Chapter 7

AN AFFECTIVE MODEL

Emotions are experienced in great variety by all people but are not very well understood. Some theorists treat them as useful by-products of experience; others consider them to be a vestigial carry-over from the evolutionary process, once useful as part of a defense system. Sometimes they are considered as motivators for behavior, and by some as sources of information about the people who are experiencing them. It is known that certain physiological states accompany various emotions, but whether the emotion causes physiological change, or the change creates emotion, or both are caused by thoughts or some other factor is not firmly known.

With such a shaky foundation in empirical research, any system based on emotions or describing the dynamics of their function must be treated with a fair degree of tentativeness. The assumptions that follow are based on experience in therapy and are necessary to the proper use of affective interventions. Because of the evasive nature of descriptions of affect, liberal use is made of analogies.

UNDERLYING ASSUMPTIONS

The most basic assumption is that emotions operate lawfully and that emotional law is different from cognitive or behavioral law.

Emotions get generated from a number of experiences, some judged to be good and others bad. It appears that they need to be expressed. The basic function for expressing emotions is one of communication. It may well be that emotions are a primitive communication system. Their presence tells their owner that something is peculiarly right or peculiarly wrong. Their expression to others transmits a message that unfortunately, is not always very clear.

When attempts to communicate feelings are not successful, either an elevated state of affect is experienced (frustration, anger) or the awareness of an emotional state is suppressed. Problems that occur from heightened emotion tend to follow a pattern. Something happens in the environment of a person that requires a reaction or response. If the person has no appropriate response available, he/she experiences an emotional state called frustration. If somebody intervenes and removes the problem or teaches the person an acceptable alternative, the required response is made, and the frustration abates.

If no solution to the dilemma is forthcoming, the frustration is expressed at a higher intensity. Very intense frustration is called anger. Anger also demands expression; its extremes are physical aggression directed at self, others, or objects.

An example of poorly managed frustration is the husband who hears his wife say, "I'm miserable and feeling unloved. Please help me." The husband replies, "Tell me what to do, and I'll do it." Wife: "I don't know how to tell you! You should just know!" Husband: "I've already tried everything I know, and you're not satisfied. You're impossible to please!" Wife: "Why can't you be a good husband, like my father?"

With no ready solution, the frustration builds to anger, and the husband either (a) strikes his wife because he perceives her to be the source of his problem; (b) abuses himself with alcohol or reckless driving or something worse because he perceives his inability to solve the problem as bad; or (c) puts his hand or foot through the wall because he needs desperately to do something, and there are no convenient or acceptable alternatives. In this case the presence of frustration communicates the need for help, but it is unheeded and runs through the almost inevitable anger and abuse cycle.

When emotions are suppressed, they tend to accumulate, with several possible outcomes. The most frequent is saving them up until no more can be saved, then dumping them (over-reacting) on some relatively insignificant happening like a child spilling milk or a spouse arriving 10 minutes late.

Almost as frequent an outcome for suppressed emotions is the establishment of a cycle—build up, ventilate, build up, ventilate. Ventilation is experienced as frequent and more or less regular crying spells, fits of anger, or periods of being "hyper" or manic.

When the person can't find a way to get rid of the frustration, he/she tries to express it to someone else in the hope of being understood and helped. If the attempts to communicate are not successful, the tension increases or builds into anger. If anger is not allowed to be expressed, it is often denied or suppressed. The person chooses not to recognize or feel the frustration and anger that is there, insulating him/herself from the discomfort of feeling. Unfortunately, the same insulation that protects against feeling bad or explosive emotions also prevents the feeling of positive or happy emotions. This set of dynamics is frequently referred to as depression.

One frequent mistake in dealing with emotion is to assume that it always results from the presence of an aversive circumstance; i.e., something "makes me" feel angry or upset. Very frequently, an affective experience occurs out of a deficit state. It's not that somebody did something wrong; rather it's the absence of their doing something needed.

Maslow (1954) built a model that indicated a hierarchy in which concern for safety is significant only if the more fundamental concern for gratification of physiological needs is cared for. Likewise, working on self-esteem (which is premium in our society) cannot succeed unless or until the need for love is satisfied. This offers a ready explanation for the seeming paradox of highly successful people showing symptoms of unhappiness while others are saying, "If only I had his (her) looks (money) (success), I would be ecstatic!"

There is a story called "The Ladder" (Kump, 1981), in which a little girl named Julia schemed to gain peer esteem in the nightly games of kick-the-can. She conceived the perfect hiding place under the ladder, obscured only by darkness. On execution of her plan she discovered that the hiding place was more than adequate, especially after all the playmates were in and she had not even heard her name mentioned. Here she utters the most poignant of pleas, "Look for me! At least look for me!"

Julia typifies the plight of many people who are hiding under ladders of academic achievement, athletic prowess, attractive physiological features, or those of truancy and delinquency. For example, consider the frequently spoken complaint of beauty contest winners: "Everybody is satisfied to accept me as a beautiful body. Nobody cares what I think or feel or even *that* I think or feel."

Another common manifestation of attempting to get love by playing esteem rules is the experience of some people, well into their adult years, still trying to perform well enough to please a judgmental parent who in some cases has been dead for several years.

The need for love and personal validation creates a deficiency in many people, who in turn try a variety of ways to earn love to no avail because love cannot be earned. Love can only be given.

One last assumption regarding emotions is that words form the language of cognition; touch and presence form the language of emotion. For a client with an affective concern, problem, or deficit, what he/she says verbally may not carry much significance. Therapists must rely on circumstantial communication (description of situation) and nonverbal cues to discover the important emotional dynamics. Likewise, therapist presence and touch may provide much more significant communication than any of the words that are spoken during therapy.

Appropriate Clientele

Several client patterns for affective intervention have already been introduced: those having anger-control problems, those relying on achievement for happiness, spouses looking to one another for happiness, children who can't please their parents.

University students are a prime population for deficiency problems. By and large they are intelligent and trained to depend on cognitive strategies. They are already achievement oriented, often realizing that past achievements didn't produce happiness but not knowing what else to do. Students frequently leave home and attend school in distant communities, effectively cutting off their emotional support systems. Students have very little power in a university setting, and all experiences are geared to end in a 10-week quarter or a 16-week semester. It's little wonder that they turn to each other for comfort. Unfortunately, many seek love only to find sexual involvement and substance abuse, which are poor palliatives for the emptiness they feel.

All of the above and many others—depressed, cyclical ventilators, discouraged, any whose discomfort is chronic or repetitive and who say, "It just doesn't make sense"—are likely candidates for affective interventions.

DYNAMICS

The dynamics of treatment will be explained through frequent reliance on analogies, just as were the assumptions.

Many emotionally involved clients behave very much like an abused child or a wild or abused animal. They withdraw from any approach; they strike out verbally or physically; they cower distrustfully at a distance. With these wild or abused creatures the mode of intervention is to begin with presence at a comfortable distance—nonthreatening, nonharmful presence. The distance is patiently and gradually reduced until the creature is within reach of the trainer. Touch is then initiated in small, cautious increments. If done properly, the abused or wild creature comes to trust the consistent, nonharmful experience and to permit further training.

When viewed in retrospect, the relationship therapies of the 1950s and 1960s were pretty much organized on the "animal training" paradigm. The counselor characteristics of warmth, empathy, and unconditional positive regard are very similar to the unobtrusive, comfortably distanced presence of the animal trainer. That therapy sometimes required 100 or more sessions is not surprising, in that the therapist became a major part of the emotional support system of the client. Subsequent evolution of relationship therapies has introduced more active interventions, including touch and active direction of the client in creating a broader emotional support network.

Another analogy may be instructive here. The client who has endured an emotional deficit state for a long period of time is very much like an automobile battery that has run down and gone dead. A quick charge will allow it to function for 2 or 3 days. A slow charge has longer-lasting effect, and a repaired generator or alternator giving frequent small charges can restore the battery to full function.

Often clients will be okay for 2 or 3 days after the therapy hour and then run out of charge. For this reason the beginning period of therapy runs better on a twice-weekly schedule instead of once-weekly or twice-monthly meetings, which are okay later.

Once the "charge" is built up, the weekly therapy meetings are like the slow battery charger; they put in enough to keep the client going. If during this phase other generators of affect can be engaged — spouse, family, friends — then the system becomes normalized, and the therapist is less important. Parenthetically, the verbal content of therapy is not necessarily significant; sometimes clients manufacture problems in order to justify spending the time getting their batteries charged.

In the assumptions section it was noted that love cannot be earned. The way to get love is to give love. This presents a dilemma for the person who has none to give. The comparison with an economic model may clarify this problem. If you have money in an account, you can readily withdraw it, invest it, and hope to return an increased amount to your account. If you have no money, and an investment opportunity occurs, you either borrow or let the opportunity pass. If you have already borrowed beyond your limit, you have no option but to lose the opportunity.

Many emotionally deprived people are emotionally bankrupt. They have no love to give; they have no credit. Therapists make deposits to the clients' accounts through positive relationship, presence, and touch, so that the clients in turn can afford to give some to other carefully selected people. These other people are ones most likely to return an abundance of love. Once the account is balanced and the client knows the dynamics of keeping it that way, therapy can be ended. The analogy casts therapists in the role of love merchants. This may be a little discomforting to some, but if done within ethical limits and without selfish manipulation, it may be a reasonably correct description.

EXAMPLES OF APPLICATION

The basic relationship-building aspects—warmth, empathy, unconditional positive regard—have been described earlier. They are fundamental to almost all affective intervention strategies. Employment of touch and directional strategies for building support systems needs further description.

As an affective intervention, touch begins with its use as a general process enhancer. Its frequency may be increased in the dyadic interview to several times per session, including entry and exit touch and periodic casual (pat on shoulder) or directly focused contacts (hands clasped at emotional transitions). The power of touch in this setting, as long as it is nonsexual and nonmanipulative, has equal value for use with clients of same or opposite sex.

If more contact is perceived as helpful, it is recommended that it be organized within a group encounter setting. Here it is possible to direct a variety of touching experiences with proper time, facility, and number of people to process the experience thoroughly.

Relative to directional strategies, consider these applications:

1. Parent complains of six-year-old child stealing and telling lies. Indirect leads elicit information suggestive of inconsistent interaction between parents and child; parents are actively interested in their own activities. The hypothesis is that the child is

acting out in order to communicate a love deficit. The directional strategy is for the parent(s) to spend 15 minutes daily with the child in some direct interaction—reading stories, playing games, crafts, and the like. This time is *not* to be contingent on good behavior, absence of stealing, and so on. Parents are to ignore the acting-out messages.

2. After several sessions of tracking, a young adult provides a pattern of social isolation even though surrounded by people. Apparently lacking are skills in meeting and relating with others. The directional strategy is to rehearse client self-disclosure in a variety of areas, to structure opportunities for the client to practice self-disclosure successfully with select others, then to assign the client to encounter acquaintances and/or strangers and use self-disclosure in creating new relationships.

3. A frequently encountered pattern is one of client, male or female of varying age from young adult upward, complaining of chronic unhappiness and something that feels like loneliness but at the same time having close, intimate, and sexual relationships at a high frequency. The hypothesis is that love interactions are being made subservient to making love (sex) interactions. The pattern is similar to that of some prostitutes whose focus is on sexual transactions and an avoidance of love relationships. The directional strategy is (a) create a positive therapy relationship that provides personal validation without sexual involvement and (b) instruct client to meet and date several people, letting the relationship build somewhat normally, with the avoidance of sexual involvement for several months. Although this may go against social norms, the "excuse" that "My therapist says that sexual encounters will aggravate [mess up] my emotional stability right now" usually fortifies the client and either confuses or pacifies the partner.

4. Just because someone has been successfully married for some time—still married, number of make-ups equaling number of fights, and so on—does not automatically insure that the love needs of either partner are being met. Sharing the same dwelling may be no more than a common launching pad for very divergent time and energy investments. Sexual interactions may be satisfying and of comfortable frequency, the common tasks may be accomplished efficiently. Still, there is often a love

deficit. Directional strategies might include: (a) reinstitution of courtship; i.e., a weekly date; (b) regular talk sessions; and (c) 5 to 10 minutes daily of intimate and nonsexual touch. Each of these activities promotes love sharing. Collectively, they make a powerful impact. It must be cautioned, however, that assigned interaction may not be immediately gratifying. It may approximate the morning and evening chores on the farm. Although it's an amusing analogy, regular milking will condition a cow to produce abundantly; regular love sharing produces an ongoing, high level of emotional satisfaction and comfort.

5. The above strategy can be modified for couples who are experiencing distress or antagonism in their relationship by (a) avoiding talk sessions at first because they turn into arguments, (b) playing satisfying music during the intimate touch periods to distract the brain, and (c) going on dates that involve focus of attention away from each other but permit physical proximity and touch; e.g., movies, concerts, plays, and the like.

LIMITATIONS AND CAUTIONS

There are several characteristics of affective intervention that may be seen by some as limitations. The fact that it is often a slow and lengthy process is one. In addition, there frequently is established a strong dependency by the client on the therapist. This is especially true if a relational therapy is the only intervention; it is also somewhat applicable to decisive directional strategies, which must be applied from a good relational foundation and must be pursued cautiously and sensitively. Affective intervention strategies often require from 6 months to 2 years to effect desirable growth. This long a period of close interaction and positive feelings builds a relationship on which clients come to depend.

On the caution side is the need for the therapist to manage the process very carefully. It is easy to permit a dependency relationship to carry on beyond the needed time. This may be helpful to the therapist's economic status, but it is certainly disadvantageous to the client.

Related to the problem of letting the therapy run on too

long is knowing when and how to institute directional strategies. If begun to soon or abruptly, the time in creating the relationship may be forfeited because it becomes necessary to reestablish a good relationship. Waiting too long creates a waste of counselor time and client resources.

Another caution for therapists is that relationships work in both directions. The process of a good therapeutic relationship is very much like the beginnings of a strong love relationship and/or a sexual involvement. Unless therapists manage themselves carefully, there is a possibility of becoming personally involved, ensnared in or even dependent on what is no longer a professional relationship.

Related to this is the problem of a dependent client who makes overly frequent and unrealistic demands on the therapist. Manipulation, like relationship, is a two-way street.

In addition to continual self-monitoring, a formalized interview pattern and location, set by the therapist, is useful. If meetings take place at weekly intervals, at the therapist's office, and during regularly scheduled hours, there is far less chance of giving and receiving improper or confusing signals than if dinner meetings, special times or places as concessions to the client, or house calls are involved.

As a final consideration in this section, dependency relationships are an adjunct to affective therapy; they do require a weaning away or replacement toward the end of therapy. This poses an additional skill requirement for the counselor.

In spite of perceived limitations and cautions, affective interventions are powerful and efficient techniques for dealing with emotional problems.

SUMMARY

Emotions provide a unique category of therapeutic challenge, with surprisingly little empirical knowledge of their function or dynamics. They are believed to operate lawfully and to have laws that are different from cognition and behavior.

Two broad categories of emotional problems are (a) difficulties occurring from the presence of some aversive characteristic in the environment and (b) problems occurring from the lack (deficit) of some needed emotional production.

Emotions are attempts to communicate. They demand expression, and if not successful, they produce problems of extreme outlet (violence) or extreme suppression (depression).

In Western society there is a tendency for people to use accomplishment or esteem tactics in an attempt to earn emotional validation. These approaches do not work because love is only given and cannot be earned.

A variety of indicators shows the need for affective intervention. These include people with anger-control problems, people who rely on achievement for happiness, spouses looking to one another for happiness, and children who can't please their parents. A special category is people who are out of touch with their support system and living a role that is impermanent and power-weak, e.g., college students.

The dynamics of affective intervention are likened to procedures for training wild animals. They require extreme patience and care in establishing consistent, nonthreatening interaction.

There are similarities between emotional treatment and the charging of an automobile battery and, also, the management of a bank account.

Two approaches to affective therapy include (a) relationship therapies—consistent, nonthreatening interaction, warmth, empathy, unconditional positive regard over a long period of time—and (b) active directional strategies—the teaching of clients to enact specific interactional remedies for their unique patterns.

Limitations and cautions center around the required length of the therapy process, dependency relationships, and proper management of directional strategies.

Chapter 8

A BEHAVIORAL MODEL

"I don't know why I did that! Even though I don't enjoy it, I can't seem to stop doing it!"

These words, or some variation of them, are so common that almost everyone says them at some time. Whether it's that extra dessert, that one-too-many television program, nail biting, or smoking, there are habits that operate without cognitive permission and to the discomfort of the performer. It's almost as though some forms of behavior have a mind of their own, but they are, in fact, being maintained because of immediate reinforcement.

Such nearly automatic, situationally controlled actions are the target for behavioral interventions. They are symptoms of a reactive style (explained in chapter 9) and are often self-defeating. Sometimes they are excesses of ordinarily normal responses, like continuation of eating well beyond need or the extreme of not eating (anorexia). At other times they are maladaptive and "crazy" from the viewpoint of an objective observer. For such responses, reconditioning (replacing) them is a major step, if not the only step necessary to bring a person to a state of positive mental health (congruence).

UNDERLYING ASSUMPTIONS

Getting rid of unwanted behavior or establishing desirable responses when their absence is critical requires a knowledge of the underlying dynamics of both operant and classical conditioning. Because the purpose of this chapter is to provide a working knowledge of one behavioral approach, the following information will give a focus on operant conditioning.

The behavioral approach to be considered is behavior modification. Quite obviously, a great amount of therapy is geared to changing or modifying behavior. Behavior modification as the title of an intervention technique pertains to the identification of a performance problem or a performance deficit and the teaching of a more effective response by use of operant conditioning techniques.

At birth and for several years after (8 ± 2 years), children are faced with adjustment to an environment that makes many demands on them. They are not well equipped to meet those demands and so must try a variety of responses just to get along. The learning of what works in some situations is the beginning of a behavioral repertoire that can be used selectively for appropriately similar demands in the future.

This is a reception-learning mode. It requires (a) being aware of some signal in the environment (a discriminated stimulus), (b) taking some kind of action (response), and (c) experiencing what appears to be the result of that action (reinforcement). The discriminated stimulus, response, and reinforcement are the three contingencies or factors of operant conditioning.

Actions that are problematic are nothing more than a response to a discriminated stimulus, with that response being reinforced. Changing that problematic action requires stopping whatever is reinforcing it (extinction) or teaching a more appropriate response to the same discriminated stimulus.

An example is an elementary school student who causes disturbances at school. The discriminated stimulus is the teacher; the response is talking at inappropriate times; the reinforcement is the teacher paying attention by chastising the student (negative attention).

A program for change would probably include taking away the reinforcement for misbehavior by having the teacher ignore the inappropriate talking. During the time of reconditioning the teacher would pay attention to (reinforce) either the student sitting at a desk, constructively involved, or instances of appropriate talk, or both.

Sometimes it is difficult to control the reinforcers. If, for example, the reinforcement for the elementary student were attention and approval from classmates for each instance of inappropriate talk, it would be nearly impossible to get cooperation from all of the classmates all of the time to ignore the behavior. A solution to this dilemma is to remove the student from the reinforcing environment for a few minutes (time out).

Because the variations for applying behavior modification are so many, and because the dynamics are so simple, it is better to understand the dynamics than to collect an enormous array of applications.

Appropriate Clientele

Before getting to the dynamics let's consider the type of client who will be responsive to behavior modification. Virtually everybody is a candidate in relation to some problems. The results of maladaptive eating habits, poor study procedures, imprecise or offensive language patterns, ineffective social skills, all suggest that behavior modification strategies are appropriate.

In addition, behavioral interventions are especially suited for young children, whose learning mode is primarily receptive and who maturationally have not yet developed sufficiently functional cognitive or affective systems.

Another group that is particularly suited for behavior modification is made up of intellectually retarded or impaired individuals, whose intellectual capacity precludes other strategies and who rely on a reactive mode of adjustment.

Although some behavior modifiers believe that thoughts and feelings automatically come into line once behavior is acceptable, this seems to be a very shortsighted perception. With people of early adolescence and older, there is an increasing capacity to think and to feel, such that (a) they have problems of

pacity to think and to feel, such that (a) they have problems of thought or emotion that are not hooked to a behavioral cause, and (b) their capacity to think and feel permits some direct change in some actions merely by exercising decision and self-control.

However, for everybody who has strong and habitual tendencies to do things against their better judgment, behavior modification is the most efficient intervention. Behavior modification is also the preferred intervention for people who are lacking in some response that, were it habit-bound to certain cues and made automatic, would allow them to be more successful and better adjusted.

DYNAMICS

There are five steps to an effective behavior modification strategy. The first is to identify the target behavior. Usually, this is not too difficult because it is (a) the action that is causing the problem, or (b) the response that, if given, would prevent the problem. Following are some examples:

Behavior problem
  watching too much television
  overeating
  smoking
  swearing
  procrastinating
  enuresis (bed wetting)
  encopresis (soiling)
  speeding
Behavior deficit
  forgetting to ——
  not returning books
  not wearing safety glasses
  not fastening seat belts
  not calling spouse when plans change

social isolation

inability to demonstrate affection

failure to take medication

In short, anything that's being done that shouldn't be and anything that's not being done that should be are target responses for behavior modifiction.

The definition or description of the target behavior must be precise enough to allow counting or measuring. Units of response have to be obvious and discrete. It is not sufficient to deal with overeating, for example; the behavioral unit must be bites of food or ounces or chews. Smoking can be defined by number of cigarettes or number of puffs within a certain time. Not calling spouse when plans change can be described by the number of occurrences within a week. This practice will be apparent in the section on examples of application.

After identifying the target behavior (each separate target response requires separate treatment), the next step is to measure or count the instances in which the response occurs. Usually a pencil and paper or a counting device, like a golf stroke counter, is sufficient to accomplish the task. For example, amount of time per day watching television, number of cigarettes smoked, number of instances of forgetting—all of these are easily accounted for. Only after a systematic counting of responses can changes in the target behavior be observed.

The next step is to determine what consequences (a) are supporting continuation of the undesired response, or (b) have sufficient power to reinforce another, more desired response. Using the habit of watching too much television as an example, both types of consequences can be described. George watches between 4 and 8 hours of television daily. He has determined that if he cut back on it, he would get more sleep, complete his monthly reports on time, and have more energy for social activities that he has been missing.

The consequences of most importance are those that occur immediately following the response. In this case the entertainment process begins promptly after turning the switch. There may be other consequences that reinforce TV watching for George. Perhaps avoidance of doing the paperwork or of some other mildly aversive task is one. He may eat while watching, so that eating becomes a pleasant follow-up to turning on the TV set.

In considering possible consequences for not watching television, it is important to know what George likes that can be made contingent on limited TV viewing. Also, those consequences, or some representation, must be given immediately after the decision to avoid TV or just following his turning off the set after a moderate amount of viewing.

George could reward himself with a first-rate movie, a special dinner, time reading an interesting book, a telephone call to a friend, money saved for a trip, or anything else he values. Because most of these consequences cannot occur immediately after the desired response, a system of points or tokens can be used; e.g., one token for turning off the TV after 1 hour, one token for leaving it off at least 1 hour; after accumulating 10 tokens, they can be "cashed in" on a special dinner or movie. These dynamics will become clearer with the examples of application in the next section.

After determining which consequences (reinforcers) will probably work, the next step is to (a) allow the undesired response to occur while preventing its supporting consequence, (b) reinforce the occurrence of behavior that occurs under the same circumstances and is preferred to the undesired response; or both (a) and (b).

With the television example, if every time George turned on the set nothing happened or if the program was of no interest to George, he would probably turn it on less frequently. Many people find that after a TV set has been broken for a time and then been repaired, their viewing habits have been altered. If not watching or turning off the set brings a bigger "pay-off" than watching, George will increase in the frequency of deciding to not watch the TV.

The final step in the behavior modification strategy is to measure the target behavior again and compare to the original measurement. If the new behavioral response is appreciably greater, or if the undesired response has decreased or is no longer made, the process of change has been successful.

Procedurally, these are the five steps in a behavior modification strategy:

1. Decide which response to change.
2. Assess the present frequency of that response.
3. Identify those consequences that are reinforcing the continuation of the present status and/or those which can be used to strengthen a competing response.
4. Run learning trials where either the unwanted response is extinguished by withholding reinforcement, or a desired response is strengthened by consequent reinforcement, or both.
5. Measure again the frequency of response to evaluate change in the target behavior.

EXAMPLES OF APPLICATION

A careful study of the following examples will provide awareness of the dynamics of behavior modification as they apply to a variety of clients.

The first example deals with a format for weight reduction and control. Preliminary information on the client included a history of obesity with excess weight varying from 40 to 60 pounds. There were no complicating health factors (a physician found no present illness factors). The facts that the condition was chronic and that the client had been able to lose weight (but not maintain a consistent pattern of weight reduction) led to the belief that there was a habitual eating problem.

In order to establish a base rate, the client was instructed to (a) get a golf-stroke counter, (b) count the number of bites of food each day for a week, and (c) weigh self each day under similar conditions (same time of day, dressed or otherwise) and record the weights daily for 1 week.

After 1 week, the weight records showed 210 pounds on the average, and the food intake averaged 108 bites per day. The client was instructed to limit intake to 55 bites per day (counting 4 bites for an 8-ounce glass of nutritious liquid, 5 bites for high-calorie/low-nutrition fluid). Raw carrots, celery, lettuce without dressing were exempt from counting. The client continued weighing and entering daily weight on a chart that was posted on the refrigerator. Charting the weight each day provides for reinforcement. Until the weight begins to decrease, the therapist may have to use praise and frequent feedback to reinforce charting. Once the total body weight begins to decline, however, the entry on the chart and occasional observation of the chart provides reinforcement. After enough weight has been lost, loose-fitting clothing, being able to wear smaller sizes, and verbal reaction from other people provide reinforcement. To make the 55-bite limit a little easier to honor in the beginning, a penalty of 10 sit-ups per bite over 55 was instituted. Also, the client was instructed to return the fork or spoon to the table between bites; this, plus counting, made each bite a separate event.

After the second week (first week of conditioning) the client showed no appreciable weight reduction. It is possible that 55 bites were too many to produce change or that the client was taking bigger bites. Consequently, it was necessary to reduce the food intake to 50 bites per day. Subsequent sessions at weekly intervals showed a relatively steady weight loss of between 2 and 3 pounds per week.

Three months into therapy the client had reduced a total of 35 pounds and had established a good intake pattern (habit) that was tolerable. Continued weight reduction was not wanted, so an increase in food intake was warranted. To establish a maintenance level, the client was instructed to continue counting bites but to eat between 55 and 75 bites per day and to continue daily weight recording. Following several weeks of stable weight the counter was put aside, but daily weighing continued with the instruction that if weight exceeded 180 pounds the client would use the counter again and start with a 50-bite quota.

Another example concerns an eleven-year-old child who watched television more than his parents preferred. He seemed to be uninterested in other activities but watched television as a pastime. When the parents directed him to do other things, he would follow their directions; but if they were not actively directing, he was passively watching television. The wish of parents was for their son to monitor his own behavior and moderate the TV habit.

It was decided by the parents that 10 hours per week was enough TV time. To manage the change in behavior the parents were instructed to buy some poker chips and give him 20, with the instructions that he place one in a container on top of the television set for every half-hour or portion thereof that he watched television. He was permitted to engage in other forms of entertainment (stereo listening, crafts, reading, and so on) of his own choosing. The initial dynamics were to "game" him into a position of making a decision before a TV show started as to whether or not it was one of high interest or should be forgone in order to have available time later. If he mismanaged, had no chips, and really wanted to watch a program, he could earn additional chips on a two-for-one basis: 2 hours of reading, household chores, or baby-sitting for 1 hour of TV.

An added feature that provided rather impressive results was an agreement to buy back unused chips for 10 cents each at the end of the week. Within a very short time the child determined that there were very few programs on television that were worth 10 cents. He began returning between 10 and 15 chips each week.

Obviously, the success of a behavioral modification program requires extremely careful and consistent management, particularly in the early stages. For example, if the child were not monitored until he had learned the rules, he could sneak in some TV time without using chips and be reinforced for cheating when the chips were cashed in.

A much more complicated case was that of a ten-year-old encopretic boy. Encopresis is the clinical name for the problem of not being able to control bowel movements and hence soiling in socially awkward places like school and the therapist's office. After checking with his physician to rule out physiological factors, the therapist interviewed the boy and his parents.

It was determined that the client was, and had been for some time, in a position where he could exert no control on his environment. Teacher and parents were very controlling and somewhat inconsistent. One thing they had no control over was the frequency and location of his messing his pants. The base rate, as reported by the teacher and parents, was two "accidents" per day with none occurring during the time period between school's end and dinnertime.

A menu of reinforcers was established from interviews with the boy and with his parents. It included various toys, games, foods, and privileges. The reinforcer of most apparent value was the privilege of having parental time and attention; the most powerful was the possibility of an overnight camping experience with his father. There was a certain amount of parental risk in including such an option.

Two formal intervention plans were initiated. The first was the awarding of points for time periods without incident: the 3½ hours of morning school, the remainder of school in the afternoon, and the dinner to bedtime period. To provide the client with some control of events in his life, the points could be cashed in whenever he wanted for small items, within a day for attentional privileges, within a week for overnight camp; the point cost of the camp was sufficiently high to require several weeks of continence.

The second intervention plan was to make the boy totally responsible for taking care of his messes, including the immediate change of clothing and personal hygiene and also the daily washing of whatever clothing had been soiled that day.

Within a 2-week period the encopretic incidents had nearly vanished. For several months there were occasional relapses, never amounting to more than one incident in a given day and not exceeding three in a given month.

Sometimes it is necessary to be creative in arranging for reinforcers. Making changes in response in order to receive that motorcycle or automobile seldom works because the reinforcement is too far off in the future. Even the immediate awarding of points may lose power if too many are required for the eventual goal. The use of parts or representation of parts of the goal object can be effective. For example, a bicycle can be obtained piece by piece. Maybe 100 points can be cashed in for the handlebars, another 100 for the seat, and so on. Pictures of the parts may be awarded and put on a poster that shows the client's progress. Sometimes placing money in an account earmarked for the purchase of the goal object adds a tangible event that provides support for the point system.

An example of creative reinforcement is this scheme negotiated with an elementary school girl who was performing poorly in spelling. There were 14 weeks remaining in school with a spelling test each week. She agreed to get 100 percent correct on the first test for a nickel, but only if the award were doubled each successive time, i.e., the second consecutive 100 percent earned 10 cents; the third, 20 cents; the fourth, 40 cents, and so on. The total possible pay-off was $409.60. If she missed the 100 percent on any test, she started over again.

After 14 weeks (11 straight of 100 percent) she received $51.55. At that time her spelling performance was extremely improved, and additional reinforcers had come into place that served to maintain the change. She received praise from the teacher, attention from classmates, and an internal standard of performance that permitted her to reinforce herself with personal satisfaction.

LIMITATIONS AND CAUTIONS

Reading success stories in the use of intervention techniques makes them sound simple to use and infallible. It must be recognized that each of the steps has to be applied properly for the system to work.

After determining that the problem to be addressed is one of habitual undesirable response, the analysis of supporting reinforcers, alternate or desired response, and workable reinforcers for change have to be thoroughly and carefully planned.

One of the most critical phases is the complete and consistent management of the strategy in its early stages. It is very easy to reinforce either the wrong response or an extraneous one through inconsistent or imprecise reinforcement. It is also easy to counter the effect of the desired strategy by inadvertently countering it with another action. For example, an aide in a program for delinquent youth was administering tokens for socialized responses and withholding them or using time-out for antisocial responses. The program was basically sound; however, in instances in which any of the youths failed to respond well, the aide expressed sorrow, concern, worry—lots of attention. She was applying an emotional and attentional reinforcer for client failure; she demonstrated more caring for the clients when they failed than she did when they succeeded. Quite predictably, her clients regularly did not demonstrate the desired behavior.

Sometimes the client will turn the tables on the therapist. There is an often-published cartoon showing a rat in a Skinner box saying, "I've really got that guy conditioned. Every time I press this bar, he gives me food."

Much care and practice is required to know and manage all of the contingencies in a behavior modification strategy properly and successfully.

There are occasions when a client may present more than one problem, each of which requires a different intervention strategy. Both affective and behavioral or behavioral and cognitive strategies may apply to the same client. The next section deals with this eventuality.

CLIENTS WITH MULTIPLE PROBLEMS/MIXED STYLES

People are often very complex. The SITE skills are intended to help therapists gain access to the phenomenal space of clients and to ascertain the various styles used by the clients.

This is nice when a client with preference for a cognitive style has a cognitive problem. The same goes for affective styles/problems and behavioral styles/problems. Frequently, the difficulties encountered by people are problematic because of occurring in an area where the people have little knowledge or skill; e.g., cognitive style/affective problem, affective style/behavioral problem. For these clients it is necessary to pacify them by responding in their preferred style while simultaneously interacting with them in the style appropriate to the problem.

Sometimes two or more problems occur for the same individual, and the problems are responsive to different (sometimes contradictory) strategies. For example, a self-defeating habit that would be responsive to a behavioral strategy may be accompanied by an emotional problem requiring an affective strategy; the affective intervention works on different principles, which often counteract behavioral principles. A relationship based on unconditional positive regard seems a little inconsistent with awarding reinforcement contingent on acceptable responses.

When such mixtures of problem and style occur, it is generally better to work on one problem at a time. An alternative to that is to involve two therapists, each working on a different problem in the appropriate, consistent style. The following is an example of managing two objectives and two therapeutic strategies at the same time.

The client was a third-grade student who was referred to the guidance office because he was "hyperactive," a label that is given incorrectly so often that it can be loosely translated as "miscellaneous problem that I don't know how to handle."

A consultant was called in. He observed the boy in the classroom setting. These are his observations of the boy's behavior during a 1-hour time period:

Not wearing glasses—girl next to him told him to put them on

Climbed over back of chair after flag salute

Banged book on desk

Fiddled with crayons after being told to get reading book out

Rummaged through desk

Went to teacher and stood by her as she was leading a reading group (she ignored him)

He backed off and stood—eventually she responded, and he said he didn't have reading book—found in desk next to his

He then placed it on desk and played with an elastic band

Talked to boy next to him

Finally opened book and started to read

"Read" for maybe 2 minutes

Sharpened pencil

Played with glasses

Went to bathroom

Returned 3 minutes later

Looked at boy next to him

Slowly opened workbook

Looked at boy

Sharpened pencil again

Played with pencil and eraser

Fiddled

Looked at workbook

Appeared to be working on it

Fidgeted

Looked around

Stretched

Worked for about 2 minutes, then scratched some on his crayon etching

Went to show it to boys at far end of row (3 minutes)

Returned to desk with boy from end of row

Put more crayon on etching (energetic and diligent for about 3 minutes)

More interaction with boy at far desk

Sorted crayons

Threw broken ends of crayons into neighbor's desk

Looked at workbook again

Stretched, fidgeted

Looked around room

Sat back and watched neighbor

Knelt on floor and put elastic band around back of chair and strummed it for about 2 minutes

Put elastic band around crayon box

Sharpened pencil again on way to reading group

Attended only briefly to teacher, then played with pencil and sharpener

Fidgeted

Seemed to know answer when asked a question about the reading

Played

Laughed to self

There were not more than 5 productive minutes of the 60-minute observation.

Several things stood out that contradicted a diagnosis of hyperactivity. The boy maintained focus on some activities for several minutes at a time. He responded correctly to the teacher's questions in reading group even though he appeared to be paying little or no attention. He waited patiently for the teacher to notice him and respond to his request to find his reading book.

Interviews with the parents indicated no evidence of health problems. The boy's behavior at home was similar to that at school, plus some directionless dawdling as a deterrent to doing household chores. The parents expressed dissatisfaction and annoyance at his persistence in asking for things. His most acceptable responses seemed to be while watching his father bowl, with the promise of money for the video games if he behaved.

Two problem areas appeared to be significant. The first could be seen in his persistence in asking for adult attention—nagging his parents, waiting for his teacher to respond even though she was ignoring him.

The second problem was a highly refined, multidirectional activity level, which may have originated in looking for emotional gratification or distraction but now is reinforced by the activities themselves and by the negative attention from the teacher.

To handle the affective deficit, the parents were involved as co-therapists. Their task was to give him *noncontingent* attention for a minimum of 30 minutes a day and one evening or afternoon activity doing something of his choice, away from home and siblings once each week. (Eventually the afternoon/evening focused-attention activities were rotated among the children.) The objective was to demonstrate, with some consistency and intensity, that he was liked just because he was a person. He didn't have to earn attention.

The second problem required enlisting the teacher as a co-therapist. She was instructed to move his seat to a position adjacent to her desk. She was to remove all materials from his desk and keep them in a drawer of her desk. He was given only the materials necessary to accomplish the task at hand. When one task was finished, those materials were taken, and others for the next task were given to him. He was told that as soon as he could manage himself with more materials they would be given to him.

The teacher was taught to ignore instances of misbehavior. She was to reinforce him for desired responses in two ways: (a) whenever appropriate to the ongoing class activities, she was to praise him for his good work; (b) a secret signal system was established between teacher and student, so he knew that when she touched his shoulder as she walked by or caught his eye and winked from across the room, she liked the way he was behaving.

In this case attention was given noncontingently by his parents to work on affective goals, and attention was used as a reinforcement by the teacher contingent on proper response. Obviously, it would be impossible to have the same person do both strategies; managed by two different people, the problems of concern were resolved within a 3-week period. When the consultant visited for a follow-up observation, the boy had been moved to the rear of the class, far away from the teacher's desk, and had the full complement of materials. His behavior was very nearly that of a model student.

Behavioral interventions operate on relatively simple principles. Their application, however, can be very intricate because of the complexity of people and the situations they find themselves in.

SUMMARY

Personal experience leads people to the awareness that behavioral responses sometimes occur without cognitive or affective causes. These responses seem to be controlled by something outside the individual. Behaviorists would describe this as stimulus control. It is based on reception learning, a pattern necessary to cope with early life demands and carried over through stimulus generalization to current responses.

When some response works in resolving situational demands, it tends to be remembered and applied to other, similar demands. Habitual behavior patterns are built and maintained by reinforcement; i.e., consequences of responses that increase the probability of those responses recurring.

Behavioral interventions are techniques for removing or replacing unwanted habitual responses. They are particularly appropriate for people having a reactive style, who have strong and habitual tendencies to do things against their better judgment. Also, for people, primarily children, who are not developmentally advanced enough to respond to cognitive or affective interventions, the method of choice would be behavioral.

The dynamics of behavior modification, one form of behavioral intervention, fit into five steps:

1. Identification of response to be changed.
2. Measurement of that target response to determine a baseline or rate.
3. Identification of reinforcing consequences.
4. Conditioning trials in which the undesired response is extinguished or in which a competing response is reinforced.
5. Measurement of the target behavior again to see if the desired change has been achieved.

Although the dynamics are deceptively simple, their application can be difficult. Complexities of people make it difficult to accomplish clearly the five steps of behavior modification.

Compound problems or the existence of multiple problems that require incompatible interventions necessitate special handling.

Techniques that appear simple by analysis often require very intricate applications in practice.

Chapter 9

THEORY BASE
An Integrative Approach

"Everything a teacher does is colored by the psychological theory he holds. Consequently, a teacher who does not make use of a systematic body of theory in his day-by-day decisions is behaving blindly" (Bigge, 1976, p. 6). Presuming truth in the preceding statement, a truly professional helper must either align closely with an existing theory or crystallize and explicate his/her own.

Based on the desire to be truly professional and in an attempt to be thorough, this chapter will explain the experiential, philosophical, and theoretical bases that undergird responsive therapy. The first section provides an autobiographical account of the evolution of attitudes and concepts important in the formulation of this method. Next, the chapter will include a section of philosophical assumptions that form the premises from which the theory should logically flow. Finally, the theoretical model for responsive therapy will be described in detail.

BACKGROUND

The process of studying to become a therapist has been a complicated and haphazard process. The particular outcome of such study was predicated on the style or type of therapy in vogue at the time or espoused by the training institution. Not having much experience to draw on, and with no systematic survey of possibilities or integrated base for a beginning, the student was limited to pursuing a discipleship determined by his/her choice or by whatever factors were active in getting into a training institution.

Many students have been faced with some professional existential crises when their limited experience or unique personal style inclined them toward ideas or strategies foreign or antagonistic to that of their teachers. Some of my experience illustrates this well. Although the theorists and ideas may be typical to the age and time of training, the dynamics are very much the same for all of us.

Parenthetically, it should be stated that because what is to be explained is an evolution of a personal theoretical position, it is written in the familiar, first-person-singular form.

As a student in the 1950s I was swept along in the nondirective, Rogerian tide. I was thoroughly steeped in the philosophical assumption that each person has worth and dignity and that each person has the capacity for self-direction and self-actualization. The logical method of presenting an environment that is optimal for personal growth and marked by warmth, empathy, and unconditional positive regard (love) was readily accepted. Subsequent reading of Rousseau led me to realize that the philosophical roots of a facilitative method were indeed old ones. That growth or progress is the responsibility and option of the client was communicated in ideas such as: "Progress comes through the thinking that the individual with a problem does for himself rather than through solutions suggested by the counselor. The counselor's function is to make that kind of thinking possible rather than do it himself" (Tyler, 1953, p. 14). The strong analogy of preparing a growth environment in counseling and the soil preparation and plant fertilization of agriculture for facilitating optimal growth occurred to me, and at first was reinforcing to the notion of preserving or enhancing the natural order of things. Then the awareness of gains in agriculture happening as the result of hybridization and other forms of direct intervention caused some turmoil.

In my naiveté I assumed that Rogers and my professors were disseminating "Truth." Some inconsistencies in the training program and contact with other disseminators of different "Truth" created a fair amount of cognitive dissonance. Here are several examples of dissonance-producing elements:

1. I was subject to some rigorous training in the use of statistical method and psychometrics. Rogers de-emphasized or even belittled the use of testing in therapy. If it was neither necessary nor advisable, why did "they" prescribe it for my training?

2. Freud, historically of some significance in the evolution of therapy, spent lots of time regressing his patients to earlier experiences, probed the unconscious for primitive unsocialized motivations, and worked to balance deterministic forces that were outside of patient awareness. Rogers put a premium on the present and avoided probing.

3. Jung took issue with Freud on several counts and with both Freud and Rogers on the degree of therapist involvement. Jung "does not analyze an object at a theoretical distance but is quite as much in the analysis as the patient" (Jacobi, 1954, p. 89). A definition of therapy that in my memory is attributed to Jung was that therapy is an experience between two people for the express purpose of change in one of them—in the client, it is hoped.

4. Adler, a one-time colleague of Freud, took issue with Freud's emphasis on unconscious determinants of behavior. "He stressed the need of studying the total personality as a dynamic and indivisible unity in respect to all the manifestations of behavior, and furthermore, in intimate positive interrelation with the social setting, more particularly the immediate social background represented by family and other direct associates" (Karpf, 1953, p. 42).

5. Rank regarded the patient as self-reliant and self-responsible—"the individual does not merely adapt himself passively to his environment; he also controls, directs, and moulds it" (Karpf, 1953, p. 54). This sounds very similar to Bandura's (1978) description of reciprocal determinism. In fact, after much additional study I find that most of the principles that were advanced as truths by the therapy masters were, in some

form, described previously and have been restated subsequently by more contemporary theorists.

6. Other sources of dissonance for me were E. G. Williamson (1939), and F. C. Thorne (1950).

Obviously there were differences of opinion (no longer "Truth") among the various theorists as to what were (a) the sources of patient/client maladjustment, (b) the dynamics of personality integration, and (c) the appropriate techniques of therapy. Although much can be said or done to discount particular theorists in light of "new" discoveries or in relation to what approach currently is fashionable, the dynamics of reasoned disagreement relative to who is correct still persist.

For me, as a student in the 1950s it was not possible to discount all of the dissonance, so I took a somewhat defensive approach and slipped into a personalized eclecticism. This position was formalized in this list of 11 propositions that I could accept.

1. The client is the focus of counseling. Counselor needs should be minimized.

2. Each personality works as a unit and shouldn't be segmented for treatment. It is also unique and dynamic.

3. The client is inherently responsible and capable of taking care of himself, provided sufficient education for problem solving has occurred.

4. The counseling situation is primarily one of education.

5. The counselor is concerned with the present; i.e., with the person as he presently sees himself.

6. Educational materials, including tests, are an indispensable part of successful counseling.

7. Physiological factors can be very important to successful counseling.

8. Because the counselor is seen as an authority figure, he can probe when it will advance understanding.

9. Formal diagnosis may be useful in serious deviation but can't be separated from treatment in the counseling situation. There is some diagnosis in every method, but it should be de-emphasized as much as possible.

10. It would be foolish to suppose the counselor can avoid influencing the situation. A certain amount of value imposition seems unavoidable, but isn't serious if it is recognized.
11. The method involves a maximum of reflection of feelings with an occasional clarification or shallow interpretation. (Gerber, 1961, pp. 8–9)

Although this was not well refined and shows an appropriate immaturity, it demonstrates both the dynamics of falling into an eclectic style and the weaknesses and inconsistencies of such an approach.

Following my Rogerian period I developed an interest in existentialism, and Rollo May became a model for me. This was, in retrospect, a time of introspection and value testing for me. After reading May et al. (1958); Barrett (1958); Brown's (1955) treatment of Kierkegaard, Heidegger, Buber, and Barth; Kaufmann's edition of existentialists (1956); Barrett's work on Zen Buddhism (1956); and Max Otto's essay on science and the moral life (1949), I was again in a position of cognitive dissonance. This time it was the problem of trying to incorporate some new learnings in philosophy with a background and indoctrination in a rather fundamentalist Christian tradition. Again I came up with a statement of tenets with which I could live.

1. Each person is unique and should be allowed the opportunity to express his individuality.
2. Each individual is responsible for his actions.
3. People are basically me-centered.
4. The focus of existence is the Mitwelt and success in this depends on learning to exist on the Eigenwelt level.
5. One cannot, even in the Eigenwelt, exist in the absence of people. He needs a certain amount of social feedback against which to evaluate his position.
6. In relation to the reactionary position of Existentialism, I find myself in a position of dialectic reasoning; (a) while I strongly favor a wholistic, humanistic conception of man, I still find abstraction and time control . . . to be a useful tool in better understanding people; (b)

while I am strongly attracted to the idea of looking at people monistically, I find the dualistic tradition an undeniable part of me; I can resolve this to an extent by looking at traits, behavior, etc., as falling on a continuum, thus avoiding rigid dualism; (c) I tend to accept the emphasis on free will or individual control but realistically must accept certain manifestations of materialism and conformism . . . and, to an extent, the fact that present and future actions are affected (but not completely determined) by the past; and (d) I share the position of saying much is lost in segmenting personality, but I [believe] that [measurements] taken through segmenting can aid in understanding the study of the complete, functioning personality.

7. People are engaged in a continual process of becoming, therefore, one must emphasize enjoyment of the process.

8. The individual determines the direction his process should take.

9. People may choose to avoid responsibility for this determination by borrowing the values of someone else or by conforming to societal or religious systems.

10. People are basically social and, if given the opportunity to choose, will choose socially constructive alternatives.

11. To have a choice, one must have the opportunity to make the "wrong" choice.

12. There is an interaction between past, present, and future in which any one can influence activity in both of the others. (Gerber, 1962, pp. 6–7)

Although time and experience would cause me to modify or restate some of the principles, the awareness that my behavior, particularly as a therapist, is an outgrowth of my philosophical assumptions still burns strongly. If that is true for me, it must be true for other people even though neither that fact nor the philosophical assumptions are always stated by proponents of the various approaches to therapy.

That the field of counseling and therapy is very dynamic,

with much variation or diversity, is obvious from a survey of various methods that have gained prominence in the past 20 years. The list would include models such as the following:

Reality therapy	Bioenergetics
Transactional analysis	T-groups
Adlerian family therapy	Encounter groups
Behavior modification	Marathons
Reciprocal inhibition	Computerized counseling
Humanistic methods	Neuro-linguistic programming
Primal therapy	Brief therapy
Biofeedback	Structural family therapy

There are few "old-timers" and many pioneers in the helping professions.

Add to this diversity the various models or theories of learning, personality, growth, and development. The following sections are an attempt to draw together the many diverse elements into a theoretical mosaic. They are my attempt to make noneclectic sense out of a myriad of dissonant experiences in learning, teaching, and using variant theories from each of the areas of learning, personality, growth and development, counseling or therapy, and mental health.

ASSUMPTIONS

Every scientific method rests upon philosophical presuppositions. These presuppositions determine not only how much reality the observer with this particular method can see—they are indeed the spectacles through which he perceives—but also whether or not what is observed is pertinent to real problems and therefore whether the scientific work will endure. It is a gross, albeit common, error to assume naively that one can observe facts best if he avoids all preoccupation with philosophical assumptions. All he does, then, is mirror uncritically the particular parochial doctrines of his own limited culture. (May et al., 1958, p. 8)

Since the primary point of vulnerability in many contemporary models lies not in their logic but rather in their premises, this section is an attempt to state the philosophical presuppositions of responsive therapy. Their validity may be ultimately demonstrated in practice; however, now they are subject to the reader's analysis, comparison, and evaluation.

Assumptions about people:

1. People are basically good. Good people can and occasionally do behave badly.

2. Individuals have the opportunity for choice; i.e., relative free will. They do not often realize or use that opportunity.

3. Maturity consists of the ability to (a) obtain objective perceptions of self and of reality; (b) make clear, decisive commitments; (c) demonstrate self-responsibility for choices.

4. Negative forces, evil, sin are conditions, occurrences, or behavior that restrict attainment and practice of self-knowledge, self-choice, and self-responsibility.

5. Most personal problems are self-induced and are self-defeating. They arise from clouded perception, improper conditioning, or irresponsibility and result in poor (i.e., stupid) choices.

6. The physical, social, and emotional "worlds" operate lawfully, hence predictably. Free choice requires knowledge of the limitations set by law.

7. People make the best adjustment possible within their perceptual set (a la Menninger et al., 1963); therefore, therapy for maladaptive adjustment is a form of education for more accurate, objective perceptions of reality (a la Seligman, 1975), for more numerous potential alternatives, or for skills in managing the process of self-responsibility.

Assumptions about theory:

1. Existing theories are reports based on empirical, behavioral referents; therefore, all contain some "truth" as a model or construct of how things really are.

2. Differences among theories are a result of (a) sampling error—not all theorists view the same subjects under the same

conditions, yet most theorists generalize quite freely to all people; (b) the model used to explain the observations—although the empirical referents might be described clearly, the explanations of dynamics of relationships are subject to all of the frailties of communication; (c) successive observations being colored or distorted as a result of early formulations of the model; i.e., perceptual bias and selectivity.

3. Life cannot be described by either pole of a dichotomy (e.g., objective-subjective, behavioristic-gestalt, and so on), nor can it be explained by one dichotomy and a continuum between extremes; however, to the extent that each model represents truth, it must be included in a more complex description of reality.

4. Models representing growth, development, and learning have one commonality: they explain progress. Models of adjustment, mental health, mental illness, physical health, and physical illness describe facilitative and inhibitive qualities or conditions that affect that progress.

The form of reasoning or attitude that only one theory or position can be true or best forces us into acting as though reality exists in polar extremes, in dichotomies. For example, a well-worn issue in philosophy is whether people exist as free beings or as determined entities, free-will or external determinism. To believe one is to disclaim the other.

A common resolution from the bind of simple dichotomy is to assume a continuum between the extremes. People are neither totally free nor totally determined. They exist somewhere between the two poles. This is a resolution by dialectic reasoning where an extreme statement (thesis) is compared to its opposite extreme (antithesis) with the expectation of obtaining a more accurate view of an intermediate reality (synthesis). Eclectic models of therapy are synthetic.

Consider another, not so common viewpoint. People exist at both extremes and all along the continuum between poles. Some people behave as though they are entirely determined by outside forces, or many people at some time or under some circumstance appear to be determined; some people demonstrate a remarkable degree of self-determination; some people show a mixture of external and self-determination or an alternation between the two. The most appropriate therapeutic techniques will be those most nearly matched to the type of person or style of behavior.

Responsive therapy is based on the latter viewpoint. It is an attempt to integrate, somewhat intact, the various and diverse therapeutic models into one system.

RESPONSIVE THERAPY: AN INTEGRATIVE MODEL

The basic structure for the responsive therapy model is a modification of the maturational control rectangle (see Figure 9-1). The maturational control rectangle was encountered by the author more than 20 years ago in an old, obscure book, the reference to which has since been lost. It states that people have a potential amount of control over themselves ranging from none at birth, to 100 percent at about age sixteen. At birth the human infant is very dependent on others for virtually everything. Ide-

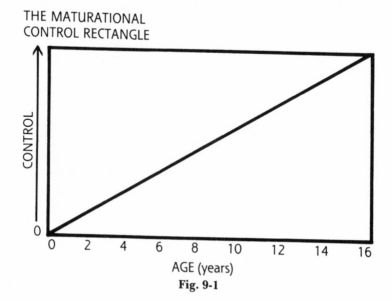

Fig. 9-1

RESULT OF
OVERPROTECTIVE
ENVIRONMENT

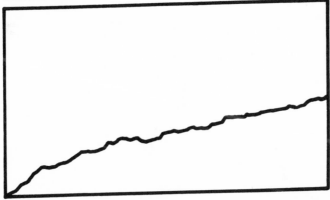

Fig. 9-2

ally, the environment, represented by the upper left triangle gradually diminishes control as the individual, lower right triangle, develops the ability to take care of him/herself. This provides a progress model of an ideal developmental process.

What if the environment is insensitive or overprotective? Development would be distorted or delayed beyond the sixteen-year age (see Figure 9-2). What if the environment collapsed early, making it necessary for the child to assume more responsibility than that child is capable of handling? Development would likely be inconsistent and erratic (see Figure 9-3).

To account for variations from the ideal in development and to provide a framework for complex dynamics in adjustment and development, the maturational control rectangle has been modified and relabeled (see Figure 9-4).

The horizontal axis is age, from birth to death. The vertical axis represents relative free will or self-determination. There is no attempt to postulate total, mind-over-matter free will; *relative* free will allows for limitations of environment and ability while giving room for existential choice and self-managed contingencies.

RESULT OF
INSUFFICIENT
ENVIRONMENTAL
SUPPORT

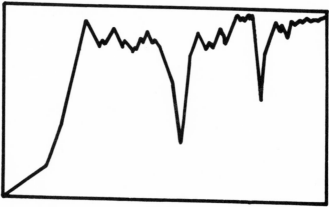

Fig. 9-3

Objective of Development

The diagonal line shows ideal progress toward maturity, which is the goal of each individual. Reaching the top line, whether by way of ideal progress or a more typically erratic line, is equivalent to the self-actualization of Maslow, nondefensive living or fully functioning self of Rogers, sense of integrity of Erickson, and existence of May. It is defined operationally according to three criteria:

1. The ability to make objective perceptions of self and of the environment. This includes awareness by the individual of his/her desires and needs, talents and limitations, tendencies and traditions. It includes awareness that there are more than the two obvious alternatives to any problem; i.e., the preferred but impossible and the possible but unacceptable—100 percent successful or suicide; rather there are many possible and acceptable solutions to virtually any problem, and the individual knows many of them.

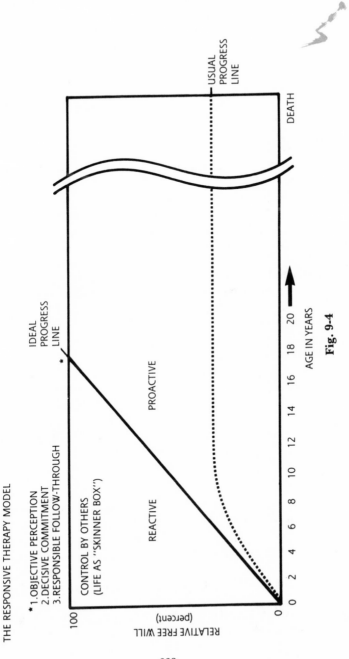

THE RESPONSIVE THERAPY MODEL

* 1. OBJECTIVE PERCEPTION
  2. DECISIVE COMMITMENT
  3. RESPONSIBLE FOLLOW-THROUGH

IDEAL PROGRESS LINE

PROACTIVE

REACTIVE

CONTROL BY OTHERS
(LIFE AS "SKINNER BOX")

USUAL PROGRESS LINE

RELATIVE FREE WILL (percent)

AGE IN YEARS

DEATH

Fig. 9-4

229

2. The ability to make a clear, decisive commitment to pursue a preferred option from among the several that have a reasonable probability of success.

3. Acceptance of responsibility for the decision and for the necessary action to assure its success. The mature person accepts the blame for failure and the credit for success with no attempt to ascribe either to circumstances or luck.

The extent to which people are limited or controlled by their environment is represented by the space to the upper left of the progress lines. All people at birth and for the first 8 ± 2 years of their lives operate or behave according to the dynamics of Skinnerian behaviorism. This area also can be interpreted relative to the number or frequency of actions performed according to an operant paradigm. For this reason the therapy of choice for all children to age eight to ten and retardates of similar mental ability is some form of behavior modification.

The dotted line represents the path of usual progress or the pattern followed by most people. Although there is no available data to verify the assertion, it is claimed that upward of 80 percent of the population follows this line.

Since most of the area represented in the model is above the dotted line, much behavior for most people can be explained and modified according to a behavioral system. To a certain extent, and borrowing from the learned-helplessness work of Seligman (1975), whether or not people actually are externally determined, they will manifest the pattern if it fits their understanding and expectation of reality.

Life-Styles

There are two primary life-styles. The first fits well the externally controlled perception—life is just a big Skinner box. This is called a *reactive* style. Individuals emit responses according to operant or classical conditioning paradigms. This occurs quite naturally as an outgrowth or continuation of the universal requirements for early learning. As a helpless infant, and for the first 8 years or so, the process of life and learning is to venture an action and test its effectiveness. Receptive learning is important, much of which fits very well the social learning model of Bandura (1969) and at early ages is very outcome oriented.

In the absence of teaching or conditioning for problem-solving skills, the individual continues in a pattern of perceiving stimuli and sorting through previously learned responses for the most appropriate one. It is as if the child comes into life with a big empty bag and commences to fill it with behavioral responses that can be reapplied at later times. As the child develops facility with sorting and responding, the style becomes dependable and comfortable. In the absence of teaching or reason to change, the style continues. That this is a problem will be illustrated later in the section on maladjustment.

If children in the six-to-ten-year range are given experiences in the process of problem solving or decision making, they develop a *proactive* style. They are able to repeat the process of scanning for alternatives, selecting from available options, and instituting an action. This too is goal directed but follows a thought-mediated model with emphasis on simple heuristics rather than behaving as a collection of repeatable responses or products of past learning.

The wise parent or teacher will provide numerous, protected decision opportunities. By "protected" is meant the offering of several options, all of which are acceptable or at least not harmful.

The proactive-reactive difference can be stated in the verbal dichotomies of actor-reactor, agent-reagent, conformist/nonconformist-free agent. A clarification of the polarity between conformist/nonconformist and free agent may illustrate the style difference. Conformism and nonconformism, although resulting in the appearance of difference, are simply valence differences of the same dynamics. Conformists do what they do *because* they are supposed to. Nonconformists do what they do *because* they are not supposed to—or in reference to their nonconforming group, what they are expected to do. Only those persons who are free from "supposed to" or indifferent to it can act in their own behalf and in a proactive sense.

Maladjustment

Adjustment or response to crisis within this model draws heavily on the Menninger model described in *The Vital Balance* (1963). Life is perceived as a flow, carrying with it many exigencies or circumstances that require, even demand, response. Not all circumstances are negative, but even highly positive ones, such as special parties, weddings, and the like, can exact a heavy energy toll. People do the best they can under the circumstances they perceive. For those who have adopted a proactive, problem-solving style, adjustments result most often in socially acceptable, self-enhancing responses.

For most people, because most people have a reactive style, adjustment is often problematical. Visualize the child going through the early years, filling his/her bag with responses to the demands of life. Occasionally some previously used behavior is appropriate for a new circumstance, so the child reaches down into the bag, retrieves the response, uses it, and returns it to the top of the bag.

As time passes, the child develops two things: (a) a bag of behavioral responses that is organized with the most frequently useful responses near the top, and successively more "expensive" and less appropriate responses going deeper, until the most costly and least self-preserving response is at the bottom; (b) a practiced tendency to look to the bag for responses to satisfy present demands—a reactive style.

In Menninger's system (1963) those responses near the top are called normal coping devices. They include behavior such as crying, swearing, eating, sleeping, and self-medication.

Going progressively deeper are five levels of "dyscontrol," spelled with a y to designate an active state or process and not an irreversible condition. Behavior at these levels is increasingly abnormal but logical to the individual as the least extreme response necessary to preserve self. The lowest level is psychogenic death.

The dynamics of maladjustment or maladaptive behavior proceed in the following fashion:

1. A crisis occurs in the life of the individual. Crisis is defined as any circumstance which requires a response that is not near the top of a reactor's bag.
2. The individual, very much as in a stimulus generalization event, sorts deeper in the bag for the behavior that "worked" in the most similar prior circumstance.

3. There is a tendency to fixate on that response either until the circumstance changes or until the individual's perception can be altered.

An example of these dynamics is a teenage girl who witnessed the traumatic death of her father in an aircraft accident. Not having a previously programmed response to such a catastrophe, she reached into her bag and pulled out her "big girls don't cry" and "you have to be strong for others" pattern. Two years following the accident she was unable to express any emotion; to open the gate would be to invite loss of control and total disintegration.

Another example is a person who had been taught to externalize the cause of misfortune, hence, when going through a divorce and for years after, insisted that the former spouse was mentally ill, would recover, recognize the mistake, and return to the marriage.

Therapy

Since problems of maladjustment occur as a result of a reactive style and the misperception or learned limitation of sorting as the only process for resolution, and since the individual is seen as responsible for his/her state and capable of changing it in all but organically caused maladjustment, the objective of therapy is to reeducate the client.

The SITE skills are vehicles for accomplishing this special kind of teaching. They facilitate formation of a therapeutic relationship that restores some feeling of personal worth and frees up some energy for exploring circumstances. Through the process of describing the phenomenal world, the client experiences understanding and relaxes enough to realize more clearly his/her present condition.

Proportionately more of the time in formal therapy is spent in relationship building and personal exploration because once the client's personal perspective is more accurately focused, he/she frequently is ready and capable of taking the initiative and achieving a resolution.

In a more complete therapy process all three phases of maturity are taught; namely, clear and objective awareness of self and circumstances, analysis of and selection from among the many available options, and active and responsible follow-up to assure success. Frequently, the therapist will have to follow and support the client through this sequence with several problems before the client can adopt or generalize the proactive style to future problems.

Many times clients will present multiple problems that in accompaniment with their unique style will suggest the simultaneous or alternate use of several different specific enhancing techniques.

It may be advisable to institute some behavioral reconditioning through operant techniques to get the client to a teachable stage. Since problems are a function of a reactive style, operant techniques will work; and the method of choice for *all* children under eight or ten years of age and mental retardates is operant.

Parenthetically, the problem with overreliance or exclusive use of operant techniques is that they simply add a new situation-specific behavior to the bag and hence do not have any long-lasting effect on the style of the client. Many clients, especially those who have a rich and variegated bag of behavior, may continue for years with little manifest maladjustment; however, those who encounter crises are not prepared to cope. It is unrealistic to believe that parents, schools, society, therapists can prepare all people for all eventualities in a reactive style.

Possibly, with clients who are older than eight or ten years, operant efforts at problem habits will be undertaken while some Gestalt integration is being achieved, at the same time as some rational-emotive work is being done on some self-defeating value binds.

Group Counseling

In many ways the previous paragraph sets the paradigm for group counseling in that the simultaneous management of diverse procedures in one client is similar to managing different problems at the same time with two or more clients. When the involved group is part of a system, as in marriage or family counseling, the added complexity of identifying who owns which problem and who else is reinforcing or exacerbating the problem is a major hurdle.

Once the individual group members are perceiving clearly the ownership of problems and the dynamics that maintain the maladjustment, they can be taught to be more responsible for their own problems or for their share of the group problems and to be helpful in working toward resolutions. The goal of all therapy is to teach clients to *see clearly*, *choose firmly*, and *be responsible* for the outcome of their decisions.

Integration of Theories

The major thrust of this book and the model described is to incorporate, in their unified and total form, all therapeutic approaches. There appears to be no need for blind or fanatic discipleship, nor for a weak, eclectic compromise. Preferable by far is a model that denotatively describes the early dynamics of therapy in a way that does not preclude application of any specialized approach, one that encourages sensitivity of intervention to the specific circumstance and style of client, and one that advocates theory-pure application of interventions. Responsive therapy is such an approach.

Summary

Responsive therapy grew out of a professional identity crisis. Allegiance to any single therapy model was precluded by the apparent worth of others; adoption of an eclectic position was seen as weaker than any theory-pure position.

The author experienced personal and professional dissonance from being trained to perform skills such as psychometric evaluations while studying a theoretical framework (Rogers) that debunked testing. Additional confusion came from exposure to a variety of theories based on differing premises. As an outgrowth of the dissonance, attempts were made to list acceptable truths, first from a therapeutic procedure standpoint and then dealing with philosophical foundation.

It became apparent that attempts to sort out "truth" in actuality contributed error by altering the philosophical context that gave validity to theory. The dilemma was resolved by incorporating all models without alteration.

Several assumptions about people are necessary premises for understanding Responsive Therapy. Included in these are the following:

1. People are basically good but sometimes behave badly.
2. Choice is an option that is not always obvious to people.
3. People are responsible for most of their problems.
4. People do the best they can from their frame of reference.

Similarly, there are premises that underlie use of theory itself and hence are important bases for understanding responsive therapy.

1. Existing theories all contain useful information.
2. Differences among theories result from sampling error, communication distortion, and progressive narrowing of perception.
3. Life is complex; singular simple models of life are inadequate.
4. There are progress and state models; both need to be incorporated within an adequate model of therapy.

The responsive therapy model includes a framework for development of the individual from birth to maturity, ideally taking about 18 years. Maturity is defined as the ability to have clear and objective perceptions of self and environment, make decisive commitments from available alternatives, and demonstrate responsibility for decisions by appropriate behavior.

Two life-styles are described, that of a reactive type, which consists of stimulus-cued response sets, and that of a proactive type, which is process oriented. Maladjustment occurs when reactors have no effective response in their repertoire. They emit the best response they have, which is maladaptive but preserves the self.

Therapy consists of teaching proactive techniques to reactors; i.e., clarifying and broadening perceptions, analyzing and selecting from among alternatives, and responsibly making the chosen option a successful one. With the added problem of interpersonal dynamics and problem ownership, group counseling operates according to the same dynamics.

Responsive therapy is seen as a functionally sound approach to matching interventions with client circumstance and style in a theory-pure manner.

REFERENCES

Bandler, R., & Grinder, J. (1975). *The Structure of magic*. Palo Alto, CA: Science and Behavior Books.

———. (1979). *Frogs into princes*. Moab, UT: Real People Press.

Bandura, A. (1969). *Principles of behavior modification*. New York: Holt, Rinehart, & Winston.

———. (1974, December). Behavior theory and the models of man. *American Psychologist*. pp. 859–869.

———. (1978, April). The self system in reciprocal determinism. *American Psychologist*. pp. 344–358.

———, & Walters, R. (1963). *Social learning and personality development*. New York: Holt, Rinehart, & Winston.

Barrett, W. (1956). (Ed.). *Zen Buddhism*. Garden City, NY: Doubleday.

———. (1958). *Irrational man*. Garden City, NY: Doubleday.

Bennis, W., Berlew, D., Schein, E., & Steele, F. (1973). *Interpersonal dynamics* (3rd ed.). Homewood, IL: Dorsey Press.

Berenson, B. G., & Carkhuff, R. R. (1967). *Sources of gain in counseling and psychotherapy*. New York: Holt, Rinehart & Winston.

Berne, E. (1961). *Transactional analysis in psychotherapy*. New York: Grove Press.

———. (1964). *Games people play*. New York: Grove Press.

Bigge, M. L. (1976). *Learning theories for teachers*. New York: Harper & Row.

Birdwhistell, R. L., *Introduction to kinesics*. (1952). Louisville, KY: University of Louisville Press.

Birk, L. (Ed.) (1973). *Biofeedback: Behavioral medicine*. New York: Grune & Stratton.

Brown, J. (1955). *Kierkegaard, Heidegger, Buber, and Barth: Subject and object in modern theology*. New York: Collier Books.

Cartwright, D. (Ed.) (1951). *Field theory in social science: Selected theoretical papers by Kurt Lewin*. New York: Harper & Row.

Combs, A. W., & Soper, D. W. (1963). The perceptual organization of effective counselors. *Journal of Counseling Psychology. 10*(3), 222–226.

Cormier, W. H., & Cormier, L. S. (1979). *Interviewing strategies for helpers: A guide to assessment, treatment, and evaluation*. Monterey, CA: Brooks/Cole.

Dimond, R. E., Havens, R. A., & Jones, A. C. (1978). A conceptual framework for the practice of eclecticism in psychotherapy. *American Psychologist, 33*, 239–248.

Ellis, A. (1968, Summer). What really causes psychotherapeutic change? *Voices*. pp. 90–95.

———. (1969, Winter). Rational-emotive therapy. *Journal of Contemporary Psychotherapy. 1*(2), 82–90.

———. (1973). *Humanistic psychotherapy*. New York: McGraw-Hill.

Farrelly, F., & Brandsma, J. (1974). *Provocative therapy*. San Francisco: Shields.

Fast, J. (1970). *Body language*. New York: Evans.

Fiedler, F. (1950). The concept of an ideal therapeutic relationship, *Journal of Consulting Psychology. 14*, 239–245.

Ford, D. H., & Urban, H. G. (1963). *Systems of psychotherapy: A comparative study*. New York: John Wiley.

Gasda, G. M., Asbury, F. R., Balzer, F. J., Childers, W. C., & Walters, R. P. (1977). *Human relations development: A manual for educators* (2nd ed.). Boston: Allyn & Bacon.

Gerber, S. (1961). Counseling—a selective method. Unpublished manuscript.

———. (1962). A philosophical base for counseling. Unpublished manuscript.

Glasser, W. (1965). *Reality therapy: A new approach to psychiatry*. New York: Harper & Row.

Grinder, J., & Bandler, R. (1976). *The structure of magic II*. Palo Alto, CA: Science and Behavior Books.

Haley, J. (Ed.). (1971). *Changing families: A family therapy reader*. New York: Grune & Stratton.

———. (1973). *Uncommon therapy: The psychiatric techniques of Milton H. Erickson*. New York: W. W. Norton.

Hall, E. T. (1959). *The silent language*. Garden City, NY: Doubleday.

Harris, T. A. (1967). *I'm OK—you're OK*. New York: Harper & Row.

Jacobi, J. (1954). *The psychology of C. G. Jung*. New Haven, CT: Yale University Press.

Karpf, F. B. (1953). *The psychology and psychotherapy of Otto Rank*. New York: Philosophical Library.

Kaufmann, W. (Ed.). (1956). *Existentialism from Dostoevsky to Sartre*. New York: Meridian Books.

Kump, E. G. (1975). (1981, January-February). The ladder. *Sunstone*. pp. 50–52.

Lowen, A. (1975). *Bioenergetics*. New York: Coward, McCann, & Geohegan.

Maslow, A. H. (1954). *Motivation and personality*. New York: Harper.

———. (1971). *The farther reaches of human nature*. New York: Viking Press.

May, R., Angel, E., & Ellenberger, H. R. (Ed.). (1958). *Existence*. New York: Basic Books.

Menninger, K., Meyman, M., & Pruyser, P. (1963). *The vital balance: The life process in mental health and illness*. New York: Viking Press.

Mintz, E. (1969). On the rationale of touch in psychotherapy. *Psychotherapy: Theory, Research, and Practice. 5*, 232–234.

Minuchin, S. (1974). *Families and family therapy*. Cambridge, MA: Harvard University Press.

Otto, M. (1949). *Science and the moral life*. New York: The New American Library of World Literature.

Passons, W. R. (1975). *Gestalt approaches in counseling*. New York: Holt, Rinehart, & Winston.

Perls, F. S. (1969). *Gestalt therapy verbatim*. Moab, UT: Real People Press.

Reich, W. (1970). *La fonction de l'orgasme*. Paris: L'Arche. (Original work published 1927).

Rogers, C. R. (1942). *Counseling and psychotherapy*. Boston: Hough-ton-Mifflin.

———. (1951). *Client-centered therapy*. Boston: Houghton Mifflin.

———. (1961). *On becoming a person: A therapist's view of psychotherapy.* Boston: Houghton-Mifflin.

Rolf, I. P. (1975). *What in the world is rolfing? An introduction to structural integration, a technique of human well-being*. Santa Monica, CA: Dennis-Landman.

Rudestam, K. E. (1980). *Methods of self-change*. Monterey, CA: Brooks/Cole.

Sahakian, W. S. (1976). *Introduction to the psychology of learning*. Chicago: Rand McNally.

Seligman, M. E. P. (1975). *Helplessness: On depression, development, and death*. San Francisco: W. H. Freeman.

Silverman, J. (1967). Personality trait and perceptual style studies of the psychotherapies of schizophrenic patients. *Journal of Nervous and Mental Disease. 145*, 5–17.

Speilberger, C. D. (Ed.). (1966). *Anxiety and behavior*. New York: Academic Press.

Stevenson, R. L. (No Publication Date). *The works of Robert Louis Stevenson*. New York: Black's Reader's Service.

Strupp, H. H. (1968, Summer). Discussion. *Voices.* pp. 95–97.

Sutich, A. J., & Vich, M. A. (1969). *Readings in humanistic psychology*. New York: Free Press.

Thorne, F. C. (1950). *Principles of personality counseling*. Brandon, VT: Journal of Clinical Psychology.

———. (1961). *Personality: A clinical eclectic viewpoint*. Brandon, VT: Journal of Clinical Psychology.

Tyler, L. E. (1953). *The work of the counselor*. New York: Appleton-Century-Crofts.

Watzlawick, P. (1978). *The language of change: Elements of therapeutic communication*. Palo Alto, CA: Basic Books.

Williamson, E. G. (1939). *How to counsel students: A manual of techniques for clinical counselors*. New York: McGraw-Hill.

———. (1950). *Counseling adolescents*. New York: McGraw-Hill.

———. (1958). Value orientation in counseling. *Personnel and Guidance Journal. 37*, 520–528.

———. (1965). *Vocational counseling: Some historical, philosophical, and theoretical perspectives*. New York: McGraw-Hill.

————, & Bordin, E. S. (1941). An analytical description of student counseling. *Educational and Psychological Measurement. 1*, 342–354.

Wolpe, J. (1973). *The practice of behavior therapy.* New York: Pergammon Press.

————. (1978). Cognition and causation in human behavior and its therapy. *American Psychologist. 33*, 437–446.

Woodworth, R. S., & Sheehan, M. R. (1964). *Contemporary schools of psychology.* New York: Ronald Press.

Yates, A. J. (1972). *Behavior therapy.* New York: John Wiley.

INDEX